THE NEW JEWELERS

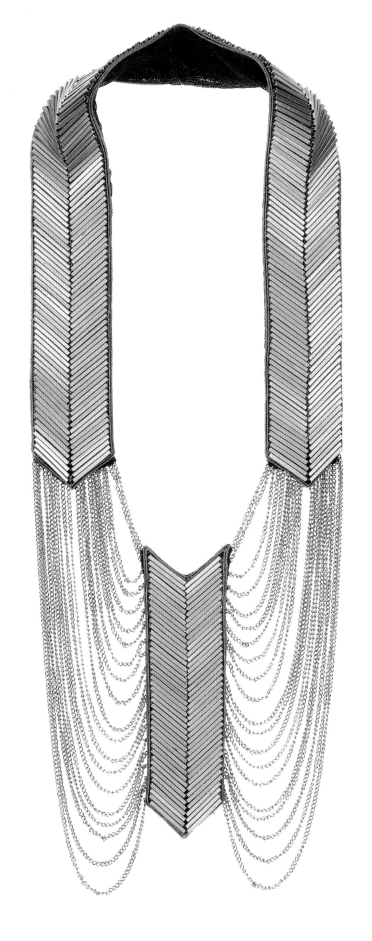

OLIVIER DUPON

THE NEW JEWELERS

DESIRABLE | COLLECTABLE | CONTEMPORARY

Over 800 illustrations in color
and black and white

Thames & Hudson

Copyright © 2012 Olivier Dupon

dossier37.tumblr.com

Designed by Karolina Prymaka

First published in 2012 in hardcover in the United States of America by
Thames & Hudson Inc., 500 Fifth Avenue, New York, New York 10110

thamesandhudsonusa.com

Library of Congress Catalog Card Number 2011946033

ISBN 978-0-500-51629-4

Printed and bound in China by Toppan Leefung Printing Limited

CONTENTS

6 INTRODUCTION

8 **VIVA GLAM**

10 AKONG
12 ANTON HEUNIS
14 ASSAD MOUNSER
16 DELPHINE-CHARLOTTE PARMENTIER
18 DU POIL DE LA BÊTE
20 EDDIE BORGO
22 ELEANOR FORD
24 FABIEN IFIRES
26 FIONA PAXTON
28 GINGER MCGANN
30 HEAVEN TANUDIREDJA
32 INEZ DESIGNS
34 JACCO
36 LIZZIE FORTUNATO JEWELS
38 MOUTON COLLET
40 PAULA BIANCO
42 SOPHIA 203
44 VENESSA ARIZAGA

48 **METAL ALCHEMY**

50 ALINA ALAMOREAN
54 ANDY LIFSCHUTZ
56 ANNDRA NEEN
58 DARCY MIRO
60 GLAUCO CAMBI
62 LOUISE DOUGLAS
64 PAMELA LOVE
68 REDSOFA BY JOANNA SZKIELA
70 SAMMA
72 STACY HOPKINS

74 **THE NEO-CLASSICS**

76 ALICE CICOLINI
78 AUDE LECHÈRE
82 EVA STEINBERG
84 KIMBERLIN BROWN
86 LAURENT GANDINI
88 LIA DI GREGORIO
90 MARGERY HIRSCHEY
92 NATALIE FRIGO
94 NICOLE LANDAW

96 PETRA CLASS
98 RUSSELL JONES
102 SILKE KNETSCH
& CHRISTIAN STREIT
104 TODD REED

106 COOL LUXURY

108 ADELINE CACHEUX
110 ALYSSA NORTON
112 APRIATI
114 CATHERINE MICHIELS
116 ESTHER
118 JACQUIE AICHE
122 KAREN LIBERMAN
126 LARA MELCHIOR
128 STONE
130 URSA MAJOR

132 SCULPTURAL BLISS

134 ALEXANDRA JEFFORD
136 BELMACZ
140 DEBORAH PAGANI
142 ELENA VOTSI
144 HANNAH MARTIN
146 JACQUELINE RABUN
148 LE BUISSON
150 MELANIE GEORGACOPOULOS
154 PATRICIA MADEJA
156 PHILIPPE CRAMER
158 SIBYLLE KRAUSE
160 YUNUS & ELIZA

164 THE DELECTABLES

166 ANNE ZELLIEN
168 BENEDIKT VON LEPEL
170 CRISTINA ZAZO
172 CULOYON
174 FRANCES WADSWORTH-JONES
176 MANYA & ROUMEN
178 MARC ALARY
182 PAT FALCÃO
184 PHILIPPA HOLLAND
188 SABINA KASPER
190 STEPHANIE SIMON

192 THE HIP PACK

194 ANNIE COSTELLO BROWN
196 BIJULES
198 BLISS LAU
200 JULIA DEVILLE
204 LADY GREY
206 NUIT N°12
208 REGINA DABDAB
210 RP/ENCORE
212 TOBIAS WISTISEN
216 UNEARTHEN

218 THE VIRTUOSOS

220 CATHY WATERMAN
224 FANOURAKIS
228 GONZAGUE ZURSTRASSEN
232 HANUT SINGH
236 JESSICA MCCORMACK
238 KATEY BRUNINI
240 LITO KARAKOSTANOGLOU
244 LUCIFER VIR HONESTUS
246 MASSIMO IZZO
248 MOLAYEM
250 PERCOSSI PAPI
252 SYLVIE CORBELIN
254 YATÜZ

256 THE AVANT-GARDISTS

258 CCCHU
260 FARRAH AL-DUJAILI
262 ISABEL DAMMERMANN
264 JENNIFER TRASK
266 KWODRENT
268 LISA COOPER
270 MICHELLE LOWE-HOLDER
274 NICOLA MALKIN
276 SPREEGLANZ
278 UNCOMMON MATTERS
280 VICTORIA SIMES

284 Resources
286 Picture Credits
288 Acknowledgments

INTRODUCTION

Jewelry is the most traceable form of ancient adornment. Originally a powerful talismanic symbol for protection, devotion or dominance, it has nonetheless never drifted far from one of its primary sources of appeal down the ages: beautifying the appearance. Its intrinsic ability to transform looks and personalities without imposing limits of age, gender or body size is what has propelled it to the forefront of today's ranges of covetable lifestyle accessories.

Whether fine, conceptual, fashion or luxury, jewelry fulfils a plethora of roles: precious armour, status broker, sentimental keepsake, future heirloom, style endorser… Only truly talented, independent, master jewelry designers can so skilfully evoke, as well as provoke, our desire and create unique pieces that are difficult to resist.

In this book I present a broad ensemble of both up-and-coming and established designers, whose ability to push the boundaries of creativity, redefine technical possibilities and figure out what sets our fashion-radar pulsing and minds moonwalking places them apart in a league of their own. They may not be 'new' to their trade, but they maintain a constant relevance in their propensity for reinvention, with groundbreaking vision, infectious passion and a unique take on their craft.

The book aims to inspire, showcasing a spectrum of design that is vast and varied. Each of its nine categories encapsulates a particular creative realm that is a style rather than a traditional jewelry codification. This means that on occasion some pieces may well belong in more than one category: creativity can hardly be circumscribed. Hop aboard with me and switch genres!

Up the fashionable glamour ante and radiate night and day in VIVA GLAM.

Morph metallic into organic with METAL ALCHEMY.

Let unconventional goldsmithing meld with timeless elegance to bewitch you in THE NEO-CLASSICS.

Opt for bare feet and bossa nova in St Barts, rejecting excess and stepping into COOL LUXURY.

Make a statement with unique 'gem-ometrical', graphic wonders in SCULPTURAL BLISS.

Marvel at an irresistible Wonderland in THE DELECTABLES.

Rock it and dare to go dark and edgy with THE HIP PACK.

Follow a spellbinding melody and be transported to glorious craft territory by THE VIRTUOSOS.

Or step into tomorrow with THE AVANT-GARDISTS.

However small or large a piece of jewelry may be, it is a portable object to which its wearer makes an intimate and immediate connection; a self-fulfilling guarantee to look and feel good. The designers throughout these pages impress and inspire with their rare skill in transforming raw materials – gems, metals, textiles, wood, stones, feathers, leather, bones – into wearable works of art that form a new language entirely of their own.

PAGE 1 Ring by Elena Votsi, 18kt gold with large amethyst stone, *Once Upon A Time* collection.

PAGE 2 'Lauren' necklace by Fiona Paxton, hand-beaded with square-profile long metal bugle beads in gold, with metal chains, *Four Sided Constellation* collection.

PAGE 4 'Megawatt Pearl' earrings by Hanut Singh, pearls, onyx, diamonds and jade bullets.

OPPOSITE 'Summer Ribbon Reclaim Cotton Loop' necklace with leather cuff and tulle playsuit by Michelle Lowe-Holder, *SS11* collection, modelled by Ana Perez de Manuel.

VIVA GLAM

Black-tie becomes everyday: the cocktail mood is pre-set.
Showstopping pieces for the urban glamazon.

AKONG

Akong defines the art of transforming ordinary jewelry-making and haberdashery items into opulent and exquisite high fashion accessories. The beautifully handcrafted Akong capsule collections often reference diverse yet complementary folk cultures, each offering a gateway to hyper-stylish chic. Bright woollen tassels, faux fur trims, chunky chains, Swarovski crystals, rich velvet ribbons, flamboyant feathers and organic cotton cords – all transport us to far-away places and recall some of the world's most compelling civilizations: the mountain peoples of the South American Andes in the *Conquistadora* collection; Greek mythology for *Midas*; and

African tribal kingship for *Luxe Be a Lady*. This curiosity towards different cultures around the world stems from the designer's own personal journey. Born and raised in the West Indies, Nicole Akong moved to the USA and graduated with a degree in fine art from Florida International University in 1999. She now lives in London, where she creates her eponymous pieces with immense flair and passion. 'I realized this was my calling the day I first learnt to use a pair of pliers to make jewelry,' she recalls. 'What captured me was that I was able to create pieces that completely express my personal style and would be impossible to find or buy elsewhere.' Her inspirations evolve each season, as do the materials she sources. The only consistent elements in her work are the crystal accents, which confer the label's plush signature touch. Jewelry prodigy Nicole always succeeds in maintaining a bold visual identity of 'ultra glamorous chic with a quirk'. Her unique designs are causing quite a stir among style gurus in the world of high fashion. No surprise for a consummate globetrotter…

www.akonglondon.com

CLOCKWISE FROM ABOVE

'Feather Chestplate' necklace, *Luxe Be a Lady*
collection.

'Bright Pom Pom' necklace, *Conquistadora*
collection.

'Fur V Collar' necklace, *Conquistadora* collection.

OPPOSITE ABOVE 'Anastasia' necklace of Murano and hand-pressed German glass, Swarovski crystal and brass.

OPPOSITE BELOW 'Marvelous Maharajah' bracelets of brass, Swarovski crystal and hand-pressed German glass.

RIGHT 'Art Deco Renaissance' earrings of brass and Swarovski crystal.

FAR RIGHT 'Marvelous Maharajah Peacock' necklace of brass and hand-pressed German glass.

BELOW A quirky audience of lucky charms and action heroes watching over the planning of a spectacular neckpiece.

ANTON HEUNIS

Confining fashion jewelry to fancy cocktail or yacht parties is a thing of the past. Anton Heunis's collections, designed and handmade in Madrid, inject high-octane glamour and elegance into everyday life (the catchphrase here is 'less is bore'). 'The ability to create something that people juxtapose with their personality has always intrigued me,' he explains. His collections, inspired by the spirit of his stylish grandmother, have a modern vintage vibe with a sentimental appeal. Born in South Africa, Anton has been designing jewelry for some 16 years and launched his own label in 2004. He began with a traditional 'arts versus crafts' idea

of designing: 'I was studying under the goldsmith Errico Cassar. We were always challenged about our concepts of what jewelry is. For a long time I made beautiful sculptural jewelry but then realized that I wanted not only to create work that could be displayed in a gallery, I also wanted people to wear my pieces. I wanted to be a jewelry designer rather than an artist.' Anton does not follow trends blindly, nor does he have a specific material of choice. Fashion jewelry allows him to experiment with whatever grabs his curiosity, be it an antique stone, a Swarovski crystal or a semi-precious gem. One key item can kick-start an entire collection. He then searches for matching materials and colours, and experiments until all the elements read well off one another. Next he develops the finer details, including the practicalities of creating wearable pieces. 'When I design, I have everything I may need to use close at hand,' he notes. 'This often means that I sit surrounded by piles of stones, crystals and components. I'm an absolute perfectionist, even though my artistic clutter may seem to contradict this.' Whatever his creative quirks, Anton excels in awakening knockout beauty from chaos.

www.antonheunis.com

ASSAD MOUNSER

Unleash the dual nature – the feminine hippie and the androgynous warrior – within you. The glamorous creations of New York-based designer Amanda Assad Mounser, drenched in saturated colours, reflect her own split style: part free-spirited and relaxed, part bad-ass and edgy. Amanda revels in her obsession with the bohemian and wild 1970s. Think of glam rock music idols like David Bowie and Iggy Pop … and their muses Angela Bowie, Bianca Jagger and Jerry Hall. The 'Moonage Daydream' collar from Amanda's *Space Oddity* collection has, she says, become 'a career-

defining piece, the groundwork for the DNA of Assad Mounser'. Amanda creates unexpected combinations of potent colour and dazzling materials (among her favourites are stainless steel bullets and agate stones), allowing individual flamboyant parts to complement each other while simultaneously clashing somewhat. What she enjoys most is 'the mathematics behind that period of flux where you are diligently trying to get the formula just right; that time of reconfiguring before the "ah-ha" moment when everything falls into place'. She worked in the fashion industry for Moschino and Alejandro Ingelmo prior to launching Assad Mounser in 2009. Her jewelry designs have constantly evolved ever since. 'Silhouettes have changed, and new ones have been introduced, but I always try to maintain a rock 'n' roll vibe,' she says. Her luminous amulets, which have featured in fashion magazines worldwide, appear like futuristic relics. 'Designers are artists,' she says, 'craving to show the world what is in their head and materializing those thoughts for all to see.' She has now set her sights on collaborations that can make her brand accessible to all. Let us release our inner Amazonian, and let the conquest begin.

http://assadmounser.com

OPPOSITE LEFT 'Paladian' multicoloured gold-plated oversized hoop earrings, with wooden and glass trade beads and brass claw charms, *SS11 Neo Conquistador* collection.

OPPOSITE RIGHT 'Rambler' agate cuff bracelets in topaz, indigo and fuchsia, *SS11 Neo Conquistador* collection.

OPPOSITE BELOW Amanda Assad Mounser layering a 'Shine a Light' bullet and lariat collar with a 'Lady Jane' crystal collar, both from the *FW11 I'll Never Be Your Beast of Burden* collection.

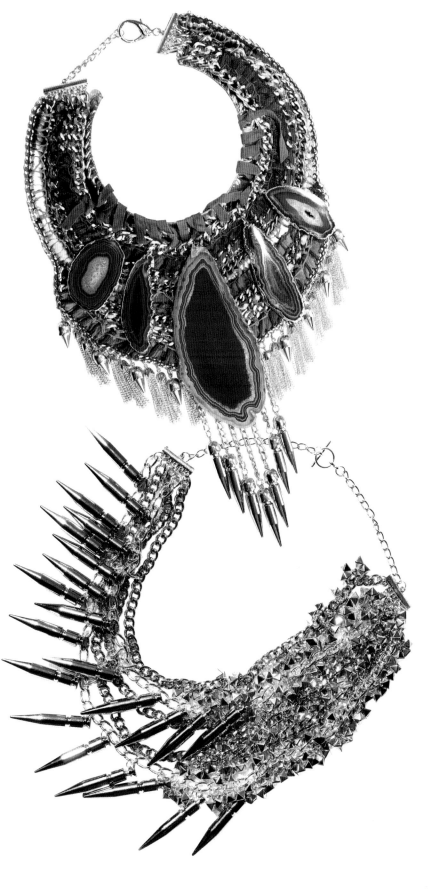

CLOCKWISE FROM ABOVE

'Rocks Off' cuff bracelet in gold with beige pearls and topaz, *FW11 I'll Never Be Your Beast of Burden* collection.

'Wild Horses Mega' collar with silk, chains and agates, *FW11 I'll Never Be Your Beast of Burden* collection.

'Moonage Daydream' collar with stainless steel bullets, chains and box studs, *SS10 Space Oddity* collection.

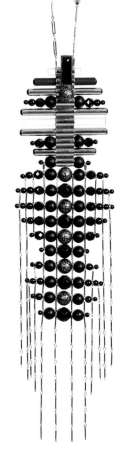

ABOVE LEFT 'Chestplate' necklace of metal, glass beads, Swarovski crystals and Plexiglas, *Studio 54* collection.

ABOVE 'Short' necklace of metal, Swarovski crystals, enamel and chainmail, *Pyramide* collection.

LEFT 'Chestplate' necklace of metal and Swarovski crystals, *Callas* collection.

BELOW Cuff of metal, mother of pearl, stilbite and agates, *Audrey* collection.

RIGHT Earring of metal and glass beads, *Ginza* collection.

FAR RIGHT Bracelet of metal, Swarovski crystals, enamel and agate, *Mireille* collection.

BOTTOM Crafting a piece in the *El Dorado* collection, inspired by industrial mechanisms, using cord, chainmail and crystals braided together in circles.

DELPHINE-CHARLOTTE PARMENTIER

Oozing stylish sensuality and elegance, Delphine-Charlotte Parmentier's collections are an exercise in intriguing propositions. The Fall/Winter 2012 collection, for example, originated from the confrontation of industrialization (as depicted in Charlie Chaplin's 1936 comedy *Modern Times*) with ethnic elements from remote African villages. Mysterious and highly creative formulas such as this fuel Delphine's magical collections. Her unexpected combos result in glamorous reinterpretations that are testimony to an unerring ability to marry different eras and cultures. Each collection is unique and, as is the case with all true art, her work has timeless appeal. 'I am passionate about jewelry making because there is no limitation in modelling,' she says. 'Every day you invent and rebuild your world.' An alumna of fashion design school Studio Berçot in Paris, Delphine has rapidly gained designer credentials, juggling her own prolific jewelry brand with collaborations with many of the world's leading fashion houses: Lanvin, Valentino, Dior, Lagerfeld, Chloé and Kenzo, to name but a few. Such impressive alliances are doubtless part of the reason she has been so influential in elevating costume jewelry to its current pre-eminence in the fashion world. Delphine sources any material that will help to create her visionary projects – rhinestones, silks and brocades, as well as more unusual materials, such as fibre optics. 'I'm particularly enamoured with rock crystal, which disperses light beautifully; and amethyst for its multiple colourways; and fire opal for its solar red tone,' she notes. 'I'll keep on changing a stone, adding a crystal or lengthening a chain until the creation finally reveals its perfect state.' As difficult as it may be to label Delphine's multidirectional sensibility, one can unmistakably attribute it to her unswerving allegiance to creativity.

www.dcp-corp.com

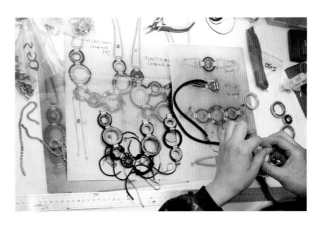

LEFT 'Snake' chain bracelet of brass and Swarovski crystals.

BELOW 'Hyena' ring of oxidized brass and Swarovski crystals.

BOTTOM Taken by surprise: Cécile Rembauville stringing beads to assemble a prototype – the stage before fitting a piece on a dummy.

DU POIL DE LA BÊTE

Rock 'n' roll couture is Du Poil de la Bête's credo. Think ultra-feminine and romantic, offset by outré cinematic glamour – a style that rebellious, modern-day baby dolls or femme fatales would just love to flaunt. But behind the unbridled, flamboyant creativity is a serious design philosophy: a driving impulse to blur our preconceptions, to push the boundaries of what can be made – leather becomes feather – and to overcome technical challenges, as in the 'Reine de Saba' necklace, whose strands of knotted pearls initially seem unfeasible. 'My background is design,' explains jeweler Cécile Rembauville. 'I have always felt I wanted to create objects that would resonate with people, which is why I graduated as an industrial designer from the ENSCI Les Ateliers design school in Paris.' After two years spent specializing in the science of plastics, it turned out that jewelry was the perfect medium for Cécile to reconcile all her interests: drawing, technology and connection with people. 'I am fascinated by looking into new styles of assembling, new technical ways of working, as well as means of developing semi-industrial processes around long-standing couture craft,' she says. 'I use a lot of textiles – silk ribbons and laces – mixed with metal, chains and stones, so that the end piece is more of a garment than an accessory.' The identity of

Du Poil de la Bête is rife with irony and joyful provocation. Drawing inspiration from the flora and fauna of Cécile's Madagascan roots, and at the same time screening age-old fairy tales through contemporary lenses, her pieces celebrate a new, addictive, urban mythology. So unleash the hyena within you – or, more literally, *reprendre du poil de la bête* – and rock on.

www.dupoildelabete.com

ABOVE 'Hyena' short necklace of brass, cotton, Swarovski crystals and glass beads, embroidered on lace.

RIGHT 'Reine de Saba' chestplate necklace of white glass beads and hematite stones embroidered and strung together, with silk crepe scarf.

FAR RIGHT 'Maléficence' necklace of black and gold brass, with glass beads wrapped in lace.

RIGHT 'Horror' collar in gunmetal, plated with hand-set pavé crystal teeth, *Woman FW10* collection.

BELOW An architectural take on jewelry from an early creative stage: sketches for the Fall/Winter 2010 collection.

EDDIE BORGO

The power of a community is not simply a cliché – at least not for Eddie Borgo, who has benefited from it first-hand. 'I owe much of my success to my supporters,' he reflects, 'those who encouraged me and have remained loyal while I continue to learn.' Eddie designed one-off runway pieces for stylists for many years until he decided he was ready to start his own business. He saved the money from his freelance commissions to finance his first collection, by which time he had already envisioned his distinctive creative style. 'My work has a lot to do with taking a "decorated" shape and stripping it down to its geometric foundation,' he explains.

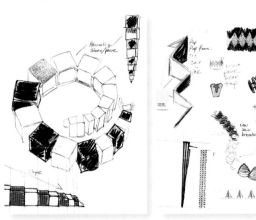

'My drawings resemble architectural plans more than jewelry design sketches.' This is grown-up fashion jewelry, immaculately graphic, with an edgy sensuality that paves the way for accessible urban luxury. 'I love the idea of subversive icons, and of identifying pieces they would wear. Bebe Buell, Cyrinda Foxe and Sable Starr – there was a lot of personal style there,' he muses. His work is also reminiscent of the city that nurtures him most, New York. 'It's a bottomless well of inspiration. It's in the soil,' he exults. Eddie enjoys the idea of combining materials that are not typically used in combination. 'While researching, the possibilities become endless. I enjoy that malleable creativity, which lends itself to jewelry,' he says. Each project is an opportunity to learn something new: the processes behind colouring glass, inlaying stones, hand-setting pavé, sandblasting beads, combining metals and dyeing feathers. An ebullient proficiency pared down to a simple winning formula. It is infectious. It is sharp. It is Eddie Borgo.

www.eddieborgo.com

CLOCKWISE FROM RIGHT

'Chainmail' collar in gunmetal, plated with handmade chainmail and sapphire glass cones, *Woman SS10* collection.

'Pavé Padlock' bracelet, silver-plated with hand-set pavé crystal, *Woman SS11* collection.

'Hinged Plate' ring, shiny silver-plated and articulated, *Woman SS10* collection.

'Four Layer Gemstone Cone' bracelet in gunmetal-plated ruby stained-glass cones, *Woman SS10* collection.

TOP 'Chunky Spiral Tassel' necklace of white howlite, silver-plated and gold Swarovski crystal beads and sterling silver chain, Eleanor Jewellery line.

ABOVE 'Large Macramé Collar' necklace of mustard cord and metal beads, *Masai* collection, Sollis line.

ELEANOR FORD

Picture the graceful sway of spiralling, cascading strands of beads that capture the light, emitting subtle gradations of colour that mimic the evanescence of a spectral rainbow; or, again, vividly coloured viscose cords that breathe new life into macramé that is adorned with chunky decorative details. There is a lot of intertwining and intricate knotting in Eleanor Ford's magnificently crafted jewelry. These qualities alone justify the appeal of her high-end, handmade fashion jewelry lines, such as poetic 'Eleanor' and the bolder 'Sollis'. Inspiration for the former comes from Art Deco design, interiors and jazz music. 'I love the opulence of the tassels and trimmings used in vintage furnishings,' Eleanor says. For the latter, decorative arts and crafts from world cultures were the catalysts. 'I adore the bold colours of Masai tribal jewelry, African wax print fabrics and the patterns in ikat weaving,' she notes. Eleanor spends a lot of her time researching craft techniques from the past and present, and re-appropriating them with a modern fashion twist into pioneering, exquisitely tactile pieces. She has collaborated with Swarovski and has also worked for Erickson Beamon, Lesley Vik Waddell and Kirt Holmes. Early in her career she was driven to develop her own signature style that combines glamour with meticulously crafted design. 'I love making

things,' she says. 'In fact, it doesn't just have to be jewelry. I'm just as happy building a garden shed or baking a cake. My passion lies in the process of making and creating a beautiful item from scratch.' All those women who appreciate delicately handmade, unique showstoppers in a world of mass production and bland uniformity: rejoice!

www.eleanorford.com / www.sollisjewellery.com

FABIEN IFIRES

When passion makes you reach for the sky… In this instance, the passion is for fashion and the sky is a tannery. A long-standing interest drove Fabien Ifires only recently to embark on a love affair with high-end leather craft. Ultimately he has embraced fashion via a nothing-quite-like-it artistry and a distinctly noble choice of medium. 'I've always wanted to create accessories,' he says, 'and it was when I started working with leather that I organically began to create jewelry first.' He is keen to point out, however, that his jewelry is more than simply a fashion accessory. 'Due to its scale and bold imagery, it contributes to building a silhouette,'

he explains. His leather is cut out, stitched, layered, sliced and fringed. Through a wide variety of complex handmade processes, audacious yet refined cuffs, earrings and pendants emerge. 'My style is redolent of the period between the 1920s and the 1970s. It provides a joyful respite that is embedded in femininity.' Fabien's meticulous expertise, teamed with an eye for pitch-perfect colour combinations, becomes even more remarkable when one considers that it is wrapped in an ethical ethos. 'I am adamant about working only with local French tanners who respect strict water recycling terms,' he notes. 'My creations are also entirely handmade. No power-generated machine is involved, just tools.' Fabien has recently moved his workshop out of his home, in order to keep the focus solely on his practice when he is crafting. This has enabled him to listen even more intently to his inner creative voice. 'The references for my work are visible, although the work is genuinely modern and novel. It isn't about reissuing past styles but about looking forward,' he insists. So much so that avant-garde boutiques have been quick to swoop down on these leather trophies, and to initiate Fabien Ifires's undoubtedly steady ascent.

http://fabien-ifires.com

CLOCKWISE FROM LEFT

'Mopsis' necklace in lambskin leather.

'Oumis' earrings in lambskin leather.

'Madison' cuff in lambskin leather.

'Chrysan' cuff in lambskin leather.

'Okiense' cuff in lambskin leather
and hematite stones.

OPPOSITE ABOVE 'Jacey Gold and Purple' necklace, hand-beading on cotton tulle fabric base, base metal chains and glass beads, *A New Start* collection.

OPPOSITE BELOW Using a tambour beading hook to thread beads from the underside of a fabric.

CLOCKWISE FROM ABOVE

'White Storm' earrings in metal and lapis lazuli, and 'Fleet' cuff in fine and heavy metal chains on leather, *Ancients* collection.

'Cyrus' cuff, hand-beaded with round metal beads sewn onto cotton mesh, leather-trimmed edges with stud fastening, *Ancients* collection.

'Dakotah' ring in hammered metal with solid framing outline, and 'Midnight' ring in metal and lapis lazuli, *Ancients* collection.

'Gina' earrings, round domed castings stitched onto leather, with gold metal beads and sequins, *Warriors* collection.

FIONA PAXTON

The ultimate armour for contemporary glamazons: Queen of Sheba meets Art Deco dancer. Metal beads and chains are intricately woven in repeat graphic patterns; regal parures of collars, cuffs and earrings are symmetrically composed. 'The vast majority of the collection is created in beading,' explains London-based designer Fiona Paxton. 'To a certain extent the technique has limitations, so this is a big factor in designing.' She finds inspiration from historical and global reference points, infusing her unconventional vision with ancient and tribal codes. 'I love visiting tiny little museums everywhere I travel,' she notes. She started working with jewelry relatively late in life, though recalls that she was always playing around in the jewelry department at the Royal College of Art, from which she graduated as a textile designer. In 2008, after 15 years of working for some of the most prestigious names in fashion – Armani, Chloé, Moschino and Michiko Koshino – she began to design jewelry. Her collections are more than mere costume adornments; they positively join forces with an outfit. As she points out, 'I think of jewelry more like a garment – the way it hangs, and the effect this can have on lengthening the torso, drawing attention to, or away from, parts of the body.' Her totemic, highly wearable pieces embellish without masquerading. Also important to Fiona is responsible design. She strives to source local materials and to ensure that the craft-making units she uses are well run. 'I don't market my pieces as ethical, but it's something I'm looking into. Everything we do is handmade and about maintaining traditional crafts and heritage,' she notes. Perennial desirability and success assured.

www.fionapaxton.com

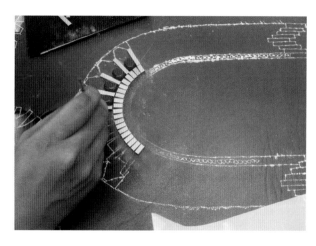

GINGER MCGANN

Art sometimes collides with jewelry in a straightforward mirroring of the one in the other, as in Ginger McGann's striking collections. This creative, Los Angeles-based multi-tasker has a strong belief in the convergence of art and product design: 'When I was a clothing designer, art and sculpture constantly inspired me. The same goes for my jewelry designs.' Her pieces are layered compositions of metal and stones that emulate her paintings and nurture glamorous theatrics: gemstones (Ginger has a predilection for emeralds and amethysts) echo sensual touches of paint, which animate sleek alloy or textile canvases. 'I start with stones or metals for the basis of the design,' she explains, 'and then just add objects that would seem unlikely to be part of a jewelry piece in order to create something really different.' Her creations straddle the line between spectacular (the dramatic juxtaposition of multidimensional textures and electrifying chromaticity) and sophisticated (ladylike allure teamed with instant stand-out-from-the-crowd dynamism). 'I began painting and designing clothes in my early teens,' says Ginger. 'Design has always been a major part of my life, and I was searching for a new medium to express myself. Jewelry excited me because it's sculptural and it's fashionable.' An inclination for all things architectural is central to Ginger's artistic interests and her professional acumen. As well as being a successful jeweler, she is the president and founder of Ginger McGann Design International, an architectural and interior design firm, with hundreds of estate projects under its belt throughout the United States and abroad. Her next ambition? No hesitation: 'To have my jewelry be as recognized in the USA as it has become in Europe,' she announces. That shouldn't take too long.

www.gingermcgann.com

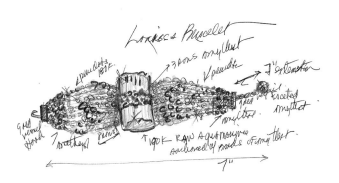

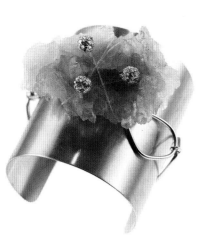

CLOCKWISE FROM TOP LEFT

'Winona' adjustable necklace of freshwater pearls and brass hinges, with taupe velvet ribbon, *Debutante Pearls* collection.

'Loralei' necklace of gold silk metal tissue, 24kt gold micro bead strands, green crystal beads, amethysts, gold vermeil beads and gold paillettes, *Seduction Nouveau* collection.

'Dakota' cuff of polished brass, brass bullet casings, pyrite nuggets, rubies and gold vermeil rings, *Industrial* collection.

'Chelsea' cuff of polished brass, natural rock crystal, crystal éclats and gold vermeil links, *Avante Zen* collection.

LEFT 'The Waste Land, T. S. Eliot 1922' neckpiece of antique crystal and Chinese jade, *The Poems* collection.

BELOW 'Finding Nemo 2003 meets Transformer 2007' neckpiece of crushed 1970s Czech blue crystal and fire orange crystal on double oxidized silver and double motif frame, *Film* collection.

ABOVE 'A Space Odyssey 1968 meets Blade Runner 1982' neckpiece of shadow red crystal and midnight blue stones on double layer and silver base, *Film* collection.

RIGHT 'The Thunder, Perfect Mind – the Gnostic Manuscripts at Nag Hammadi in 1945' neckpiece of Venetian antique chandelier crystal, 1920s French jet and crystal, *The Poems* collection.

HEAVEN TANUDIREDJA

Heaven Tanudiredja's career traces a spiritual journey … the kind that is driven by the creative urge of a visionary who believes that 'worn jewelry represents the soul of a person, while the clothes represent their ambition'. Born in Jakarta, Heaven has been working since he was 14 years old, initially as an assistant tailor after school hours. At the age of 16 he began studying fashion design, which kick-started a meteoric learning curve: 'My first boss in Indonesia, Biyan, taught me what it is to be a designer,' he recalls. 'When I was studying at the Royal Academy of Fine Arts in Antwerp, I learned to develop my personality. Later, with John Galliano at Christian Dior, I discovered freedom of creativity. Then, with Dries Van Noten, I improved my focus and learnt to appreciate the importance of dignity.' These experiences have helped Heaven to evolve a unique creative identity. His spectacular works evoke the gleaming heraldic emblems of futuristic yet romantic goddesses. Each creation is the expression of meticulous craftwork that strives to achieve the ultimate in desirable organic luxury. Heaven's gloriously elaborate pieces are handmade in his Antwerp studio, using organic textiles where possible. This is a difficult task given the scarcity of some of the materials he uses, such as antique crystals and natural lacquer from Japan. 'Brainstorming with my team is essential to our creative process; the impetus to any new idea, to research and to new techniques,' he insists. 'Once a collection is finished, we have to move on to the next one.' His dream project would be to fashion an immense piece of jewelry – a necklace sculpture, 100 metres long by 10 metres wide, which would sit beneath the Northern Lights in Norway. As extraordinary as it sounds, it has all the hallmarks of a dream that will come true.

www.heaventanudiredja.be

INEZ DESIGNS

If you want something done well, do it yourself … or so the saying goes. But it doesn't also suggest that it should be done in high style. So when a truly creative spirit like Inez Tan tackles the lack of appropriate fashion jewelry for her own needs by handcrafting unique 'vintage meets bling' neck-dresses and rings, the results are breathtaking. Inez is a Singaporean self-taught enchanter, who took up the challenge of converting her fashion design skills to create elaborate costume jewelry. Several years ago she needed an accessory to go with an outfit and decided to craft something from vintage buttons and scraps of fabric that were lying around. The rest is history. 'My work is challenging,' she points out, 'because I don't have jewelry skills. If a technique isn't working out, I have to think of an alternative. That's the price I have to pay. My pieces are all handmade and I aspire to quality and unconventionality. As a result, each piece takes a long time to make.' The crafting process is similar to that of a seamstress making a pattern. Inez starts by selecting a template shape, pinning it on felt and then covering it with a layer of tulle. 'I then start adding beads, rhinestones, silk, lace or rare vintage details. It's like embedding a story into each piece, so that every creation is different and has its own personality,' she says. The *Flora, Fauna and a bit of Tribal* collection, in particular, conveys the über-decorative impact and one-of-a-kind, handcrafted refinement that are the hallmarks of Inez Designs. Features such as these deservedly position the eye-catching designs of this exciting young brand as essential components of any confident wardrobe.

http://inez-designs.com

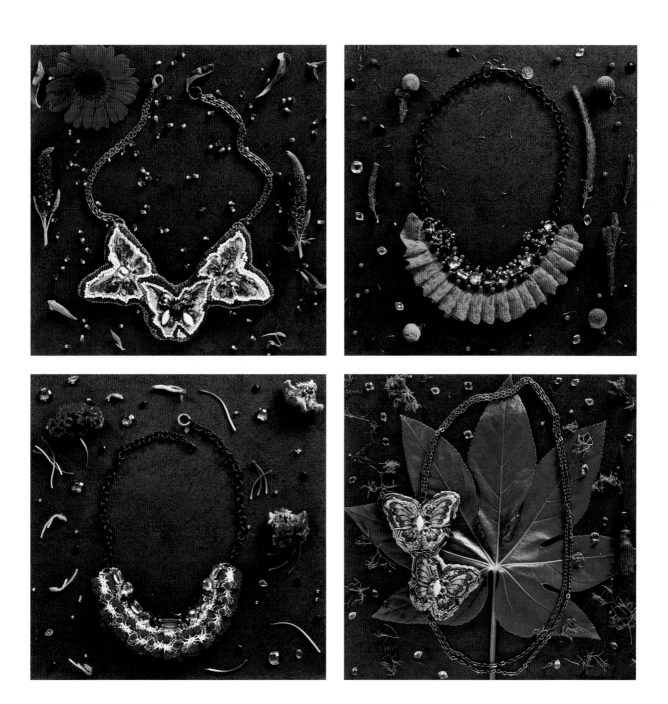

TOP LEFT 'Embroidery Colored Butterfly' necklace, *Flora, Fauna and a bit of Tribal* collection.

ABOVE LEFT 'Vintage Red Trims' necklace, *Flora, Fauna and a bit of Tribal* collection.

TOP RIGHT 'Vintage Orange Trims' necklace, *Flora, Fauna and a bit of Tribal* collection.

ABOVE RIGHT 'Embroidery Decay Butterfly Gems' necklace, *Flora, Fauna and a bit of Tribal* collection.

JACCO

Board a peaceful houseboat floating somewhere north of Paris and enter Sawako Ishitani's laboratory of ideas… Fashion jewelry, extraordinary for its innovative quirks as much as its otherworldly narratives, adorns a dishevelled yet futuristic Marie Antoinette figure, whose oversized, puffy hairdo seems to imply that her head floats in the clouds. This dreamlike vision materialized at the start of Sawako's career. Each subsequent collection has evolved from a backdrop of historical references and fictional tales, and its final visual *mise en scène* is integral to the creative process. 'First I decide the character or theme of the collection,' she explains. 'It

may begin with a shapeless vision, or perhaps just a keyword. After the main concept has been decided, I envisage different sub-series within the collection. Each series is unique, even though it remains cohesive in terms of the overall ensemble.' Sawako studied sculpture and contemporary art in Japan. She left at the age of 18 to travel the world, finally settling in Paris, where she worked as an accessory designer for various well-known fashion houses before launching JACCO, so-called after her childhood nickname (the word for a small fish in Japan). 'I can express my artistic concepts and emotions most easily in an object like jewelry, which is also deeply connected to women's desire,' says Sawako. 'Since I've been running my own label, I can say that it's more about myself than ever.' However, she also notes, 'I shouldn't feel that "This is it; I have a creative style!" Never be afraid to change the image, because that is what makes the style.' Appealing girly rock glamour and offbeat playfulness exude from each sautoir necklace and intricate earring, so much so that it is difficult not to exclaim, 'Oh … I want a bite!'

www.jacco-jacco.com

OPPOSITE ABOVE 'No. 280' earrings in 24kt gold-plated brass, *K* collection.

OPPOSITE BELOW Floating in creativity: the peaceful and poetic surroundings of Sawako Ishitani's houseboat workshop.

CLOCKWISE FROM ABOVE

'Cowgirl Deluxe' necklace of 24kt gold-plated brass, resin and aluminium beads, *Cosmo* collection.

'Candy Cane Madeleine' bracelet of resin and Bohemian glass beads, with silver-plated brass charm, *Gato* collection.

'Arrow Heart' necklace of 18kt gold-plated brass, 24kt gold-plated arrow charms and Bohemian glass beads, *Gretel* collection.

LEFT 'Medicine Woman II' necklace, hand-beaded on looms, with forest green and red 'Navajo'-print patch on brass box chain, gold bead detail and black suede fringe, *Old Laughing Lady* collection.

BELOW The India-inspired Spring/Summer 2010 collection in preparation, with Lizzie Fortunato's own cross-stitching samples and fabric swatches.

OPPOSITE ABOVE LEFT 'Old Laughing Lady' necklace of soldered antique gold-plated brass chain woven with leather, silk thread and amethysts, black feather trim, *Old Laughing Lady* collection.

OPPOSITE ABOVE RIGHT 'Layla' necklace of hand-knotted and stuffed Liberty print 'knots', African glass beads, brass beads, African opals and coral, leather closure, *Long Live Summer* collection.

LIZZIE FORTUNATO JEWELS

Jewelry and leather accessory making as script writing. This is the mantra that sets Lizzie Fortunato Jewels apart. Working from a charming New York City studio, Lizzie and her twin sister, Kathryn, are the label's dream team: Lizzie is the creative force, while Kathryn runs the business side. 'Each season I envisage the girl who would be wearing the particular collection. This character development helps to inspire the styles,' Lizzie explains. 'I am always striving to create something that is both classic and a statement. I try to achieve designs that would suit my grandmother as well as my twenty- and thirty-something best friends.' Somewhat unconventionally, there are no signature pieces that are repeated season after season. Instead, there are 'signature silhouettes' that show up in different materials or colourways across the seasons. 'We follow more of a ready-to-wear model, showing distinct collections each season,' Lizzie states. Noticeably, the use of artisanal handicraft and needlework helps to transform 'lowbrow' materials – ropes, cast bolts, spools of leather, feathers – into 'highbrow', fashion-forward designs. Lizzie's commitment to drawing inspiration and materials from a seemingly inexhaustible stockpile of sources is one of the brand's defining (and competitive) features. From an extraordinary silk ribbon in a midtown-Manhattan trimmings shop to exotic materials and fortuitous finds, Lizzie clearly has a keen eye for rarities and quirks that will embellish her stories. 'People love to know the history behind the piece they're wearing, particularly if it was a casino-chip-turned-pendant that may once have been in the hands of a South American playboy,' she laughs. Besides, customers often say that when they are not wearing their Lizzie Fortunato necklace it is hanging on the wall or displayed on a vanity table. Iconographic fashion accessories symbolize artful mementoes.

http://lizziefortunatojewels.com

BOTTOM LEFT 'The Secret Hero of These Poems' necklace of braided binding and industrial brass chain, hand-sewn silk ikat, cotton, linen rosettes, vintage woven buttons, peace sign charms, brass beads, white mother of pearl, opal beads and large lemon opals, brass closure, *Long Live Summer* collection.

BOTTOM RIGHT 'Floreana' necklace of gold-plated brass box chain, labradorite beads, woven embroidery, tassels, vintage Czech glass, rhodonite and gold-plated brass bullet charms, *Paradise is an Island* resort collection.

MOUTON COLLET

Mouton Collet has introduced a new sensual vocabulary, a visual poetry, into the world of fashion. The collections for men and women follow the creative journey of the brand's founders, Matthieu Mouton and Nicolas Collet. 'Our accessories are the well crafted and atypical "full stops" of any silhouette,' they explain. 'Our creative path is artistic, yet the results are to be worn proudly. It is more a visual than an intellectual statement.' Their teamwork thrives on 'curiosity and dualities: force versus fragility, beauty versus ugliness, reality versus surrealism'. After meeting at the Institut Saint-Luc Tournai in Belgium, they 'rushed' to Paris, where they launched their brand in 2005, while collaborating with luminaries such as Martin Margiela, Loulou de la Falaise, Hervé Léger, Jitrois, Kenzo, Nina Ricci by Olivier Theyskens and A. F. Vandervorst. These invaluable experiences forged their grasp of luxury fashion, but perhaps the most significant collaboration was the phantasmagorical helmet with fur and horns they created for Lady Gaga's 'Alejandro' video, directed by Steven Klein. This contributed as much to the pop icon's edgy fashion notoriety as to Mouton Collet's place in today's hype design scene. Their creative process starts with intense, almost volcanic, storytelling – according to them, 'delving into chimerical waters, a near religious experience'. Subsequent revelations are filtered through their own modern vision, sketched and allocated materials (silver and enamel are firm favourites), then sampled and turned into playful, colour-saturated, part pop glam/part punk rock, highly covetable jewelry and accessory stunners. Mouton Collet celebrates otherworldly and slightly ferocious flora and fauna. It creates designs for audacious, fashion-driven individuals who flaunt their style unashamedly. 'It is about seeking attention, but it's mostly about appealing to oneself,' they proclaim. Amen.

www.moutoncollet.com

ABOVE 'Trophée de Chasse' headband, with real hunt trophy lacquered in black, satin ribbon and glass bead embroidery, *Féroce* collection.

ABOVE RIGHT 'Alejandro' helmet in sequinned tar-plated Plexiglas with silver metal spikes and gourmette chain, *Bords de Mer* collection.

RIGHT 'Bouton d'Or' earrings of brass beads, gourmette chain and copper finishing, *Vénéneuse* collection.

CLOCKWISE FROM RIGHT

'Victory' one-off necklace of clear, varnished and painted wood cubes, Plexiglas plates, black screws and laser-cut gold-plated brass letters inspired by salvaged wooden letter fonts.

'Nugget' dark silver-plated earrings of vintage Swarovski octagonal crystal, crystal beads and tassel chains.

'Alice After Party' one-off headband with gold-plated frame and broken porcelain pieces from traditional English, Bukharan and Delft china.

Stack of three bracelets of Swarovski crystals and gourmette chain hand-wrapped with satin silk fabric.

RIGHT 'Eve' necklace of hand-cut chiffon flowers, Swarovski pearls nestled inside each, black silver-plated chain.

BELOW Smadar-Pola Azriel wrapping fabric around Swarovski crystals to line a bracelet frame (as in the bracelets seen opposite).

PAULA BIANCO

Attention please! The curtain goes up to reveal a stage adorned with ravishing creations that showcase unexpected combinations of crystals, beads, porcelain, soft airy fabrics and other materials. Israeli designer Smadar-Pola Azriel likens wearing a piece of jewelry while it is still in progress to putting on a dress rehearsal, and then the donning of the magnificent finished piece to stepping out on stage with a bang ... a Paula Bianco revelation! For Smadar-Pola, building a new collection is a poetic enterprise. 'Clothing fabric is not a classic jewelry material, but it is an outstandingly beautiful companion to metal, and one that brings femininity

and lyricism to the whole story.' It was after a few years working as a successful interior designer that Smadar-Pola embarked on a career as a jewelry designer. This was the perfect medium for her two great passions, fashion and design. 'Jewelry is the icing on the cake,' she states. 'Wearing jewelry allows me either to be noticed or not, simply by putting on a statement piece or switching to something more subdued.' She is self-taught and therefore enlisted the help of goldsmiths to incorporate traditional techniques with unconventional materials. And eventually her complex visions materialized. In the *Cube* collection, for example, she managed to convert functional items – wooden block-print letters – into artistic attire by using modern techniques, yet without losing the original, authentic feel. 'I had to work with a variety of professionals who essentially have nothing whatsoever to do with jewelry design: carpenters, engravers and a laser-cutting factory,' she explains. 'My ideas for designs are always triggered when I want to wear something that doesn't exist.' Long may Smadar-Pola continue to bring her reveries to life and to us!

www.paulabianco.com

SOPHIA 203

A life-changing encounter set the creative ball rolling for the Swedish designer Sophia Edstrand. While living in India and working with the renowned French jeweler Marie-Hélène de Taillac, Sophia was exposed to the remarkable traditions of Indian handicraft. Then she discovered a technique that would rock her world: 'I never wanted to have my own brand until I stumbled upon a rare embroidery technique while browsing in the bazaars of Jaipur,' she enthuses. Soon thereafter Sophia 203 was born – a joyful collection of graphic accessories, blazing with colour and conjuring up a spirit of youthful spontaneity. Drawing inspiration from vintage jewelry, Sophia first works on her motifs, sketching full-scale paper representations to mock up the proportions of a belt or show how a necklace will sit on the neck. 'I then choose the colours, playing with hundreds of silk tassels. Next the embroiderers copy my artwork. They make small samples, we decide which techniques work best for the different motifs, then they proceed with the full piece.' Enchanting details, from hearts and butterflies to shells and peonies, adorn a wide range of accessories, including headbands, collars, brooches, shoes and belts. The fun-loving vibe is offset by the lustrous elegance of the core material, silk. It is this that makes Sophia 203 a distinctly grown-up proposition. 'I love the luminosity of the silk threads,' she says, 'and the technique I've developed delivers a beautiful texture.' The thought of someone buying her work just because they love it fills Sophia with delight. 'It's a luxury to make things that don't need to perform a function,' she confesses. That said, we can think of innumerable functions for Sophia 203 creations – not least of which is putting a smile on your face, or simply making the world a more exhilarating place to be.

www.sophia203.com

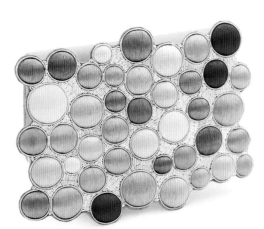

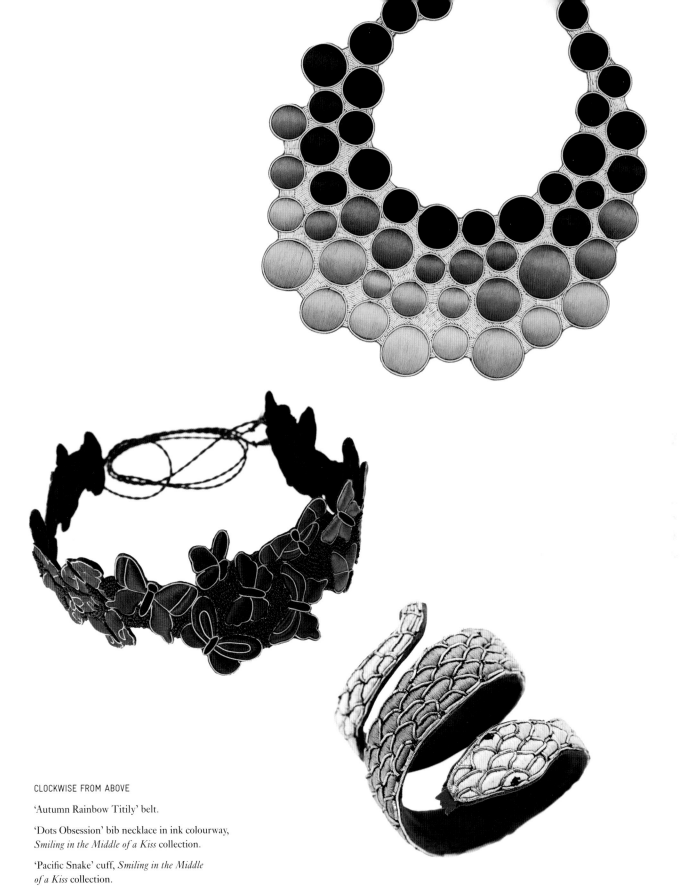

CLOCKWISE FROM ABOVE

'Autumn Rainbow Titily' belt.

'Dots Obsession' bib necklace in ink colourway,
Smiling in the Middle of a Kiss collection.

'Pacific Snake' cuff, *Smiling in the Middle
of a Kiss* collection.

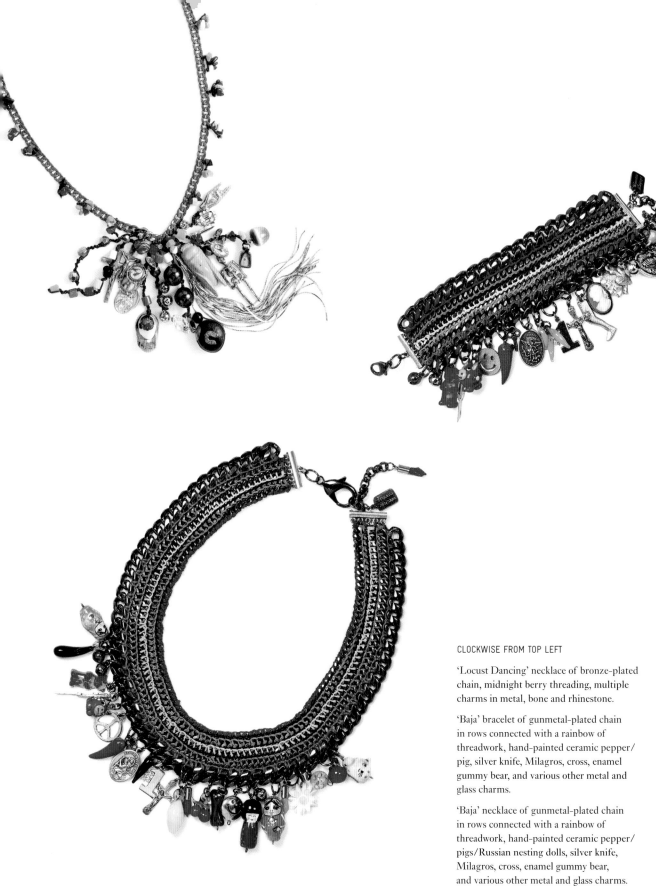

CLOCKWISE FROM TOP LEFT

'Locust Dancing' necklace of bronze-plated chain, midnight berry threading, multiple charms in metal, bone and rhinestone.

'Baja' bracelet of gunmetal-plated chain in rows connected with a rainbow of threadwork, hand-painted ceramic pepper/ pig, silver knife, Milagros, cross, enamel gummy bear, and various other metal and glass charms.

'Baja' necklace of gunmetal-plated chain in rows connected with a rainbow of threadwork, hand-painted ceramic pepper/ pigs/Russian nesting dolls, silver knife, Milagros, cross, enamel gummy bear, and various other metal and glass charms.

RIGHT 'High Tide' necklace of silver-plated chain with lemon threadwork, glass pearls, hand-painted ceramic skulls, black wooden skulls with diamond rhinestone eyes, silver-plated cross, acrylic cartoon bird heart, resin-cast gummy bear and various other elements.

BELOW Venessa Arizaga's mood board attests to her rock 'n' roll/ethnic vibe and showcases her passion for intricate knotting and threading templates.

VENESSA ARIZAGA

Bif! Bam! Pow! Dazzling with psychedelic colours and laden with good-luck charms, Venessa Arizaga's costume jewelry will unleash your inner fashion superhero in truly brazen style. The technique she applies to her work is in itself no mean feat: the limited scope of metal chains is offset by the seemingly infinite possibilities of threading, which Venessa revels in exploring to the full. Intricate weaving patterns compose 'rainbow on acid' pictures, while voodooish yet cheerful trinkets confer a 3D extravaganza. 'I use threading in all my pieces. It's a gorgeous, high-quality threading manufactured in Germany that comes in hundreds of colours,

weights and twists,' she explains. 'The most magical aspect of it is the endless permutation of colours and textures one can create.' Venessa realized early in her career that threads could be just as durable as metal. Fuelled by an unbridled imagination, she stepped out of her comfort zone to challenge weights, chain combinations and sewing materials in Manga meets South America cock-a-hoops. A graduate of Parsons design school in New York, Venessa was a fashion designer for Tuleh and Carolina Herrera, and the design director for Zac Posen, before deciding to turn her jewelry making – a hobby at first – into a fully fledged career. 'My creative style is all over the place,' she confesses. 'I feel like a mad scientist! It's quite normal for me to have pots of dye boiling, an inspiration wall with hundreds of notes scattered about, and swatches on every inch of the table. I like to work on several different projects at a time because it enables me to see everything as a complete idea.' The dream project? Venessa fantasizes about collaborating on 'the most gorgeous Chanel suits dripping with my work'. Picture that!

http://venessaarizaga.com

TOP 'Woodstock' bracelet of gunmetal-plated chain in rows connected with a rainbow of threadwork, hand-painted ceramic skulls, silver peace sign, gold knife, and various glass, metal and ceramic charms.

CENTRE 'Laser Eyes' bracelet in orange, red, lime green, black and white needlepoint on leather backing, depicting an Asian girl's eyes, with diamond rhinestone trim.

ABOVE 'Psycho Mayan' bracelet of multi-rainbow embroidered threads, hand-painted ceramic skulls and glass rhinestones.

ABOVE 'Piñata' bracelet of silver-plated chain,
lapis threading, multiple charms in metal, shell,
rhinestone and ceramic, hand-painted cameos.

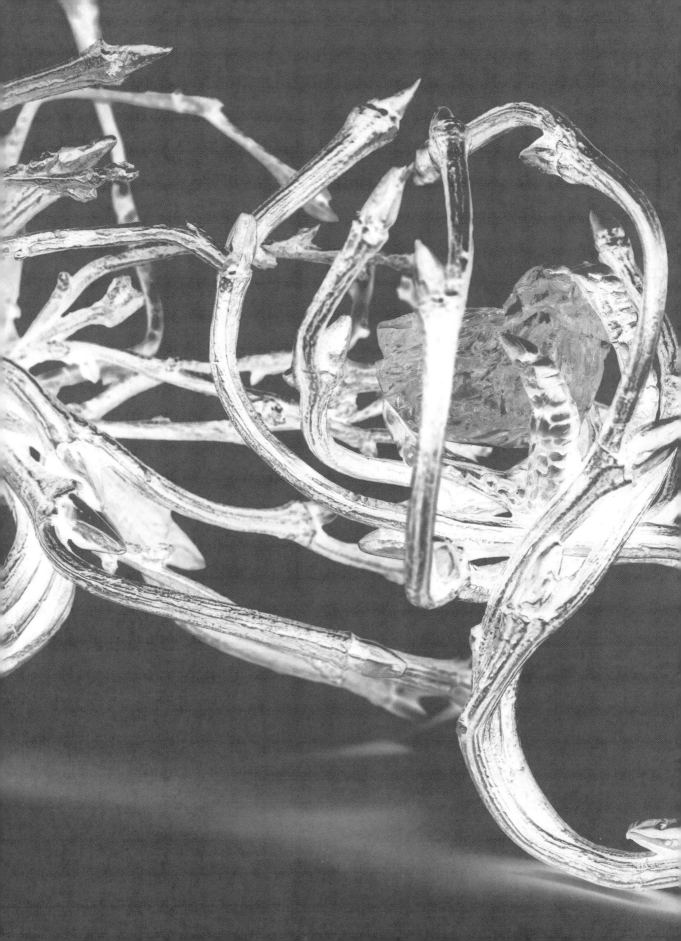

METAL ALCHEMY

Second-skin talismanic armour to adorn the body with powerful beauty.
Alloy has never felt so sensually enthralling.

ALINA ALAMOREAN

What if emptiness is as important as solidity? This approach to design, essential for architects, is inherent in Alina Alamorean's creations. Her small-scale yet bold pieces are sculptures, boasting both fluidity and rigour. With their robust surfaces and sensual volumes, they have the air of monumental installations. 'When caressing the smooth polished outline of my rings,' she whispers, 'it feels like touching the beautiful lines of the body you love.' Romanian-born Alina, the daughter of two architects, has been designing jewelry since she was a teenager and describes her current

designs as minimalist in style yet dramatic and rebellious in intent. 'I try to say something with one single torsion of the metal, and with no soldering, if possible. I wish I could materialize an idea without any material support. Air is a luxury that architects understand well.' Alina graduated in jewelry from the École de la Rue du Louvre. In 2007 she won the most prestigious prize in the contemporary jewelry world, the HRD International Diamonds Award, for which she has been nominated twice. She has also won the special prize at the Tahitian Pearl Trophy awards, and been nominated twice for the Grand Prix de la Création de la Ville de Paris. Having nurtured constructive collaborations with private galleries and clients, the free-spirited Alina has also developed an appreciation of the importance of fate. 'I tend not to control the surface of my jewelry and just see what happens. There is a mystery and wonder in witnessing the life and soul of the metal emerging.' Rather than decoration and detail, she embraces the core substance of her designs – extensions of her visceral way of being and feeling. 'Some people are afraid of my jewelry,' she remarks. 'They think it's aggressive; that my rings are weapons.' How could anyone not see that they are in fact declarations of love?

www.alina-alamorean.com

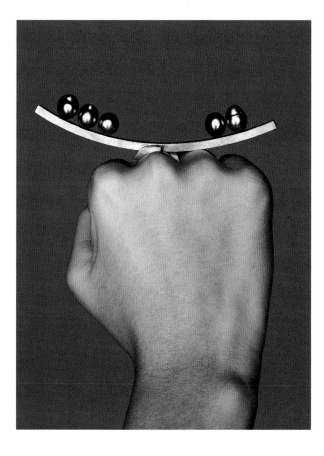

CLOCKWISE FROM TOP LEFT

'Les Moineaux' ring in silver with Tahitian pearls.

'Les Moineaux' pendant necklace in silver with
Tahitian pearls.

'Big Dragon' ring in silver.

'Rough Diamonds' rings in silver, with bronze and
with white rough diamonds.

ABOVE 'Big Choker' necklace in 900 silver and saddle-stitched leather.

LEFT 'Bulles de Poison' rings in silver with Tahitian pearls.

ABOVE Three views of 'The Eye of the Devil'
ring of silver, 50ct rhodolite garnet and
white brilliant-cut diamonds.

RIGHT 'Wings of Desire' ring in silver.

ANDY LIFSCHUTZ

Ready to be swept away with awe and consumed by desire? As one spellbound client of Andy Lifschutz explains: 'His work carries such emotional value with it. The piece that I purchased brought me to tears when I first saw it.' It is as if each of his works channels his passion for his craft and takes charge of the wearer's own sensory perceptions. Andy's artisanship is evident in his meticulous metalwork, which pushes the lustrous element to its absolute limits. But he is also an alchemist, sourcing striking raw gems and crystals to adorn his rings, and then transforming them into objects that resemble great flames from torches belonging to gods of the underworld. The narrative of his creations mirrors his own unfolding life story. US-based Andy expresses himself fully through his art: 'The ability to translate life experience into wearable adornment is a drive. My creations tell stories and draw influence from my own history. As I continue to explore my existence, my work progresses along with it,' he explains. 'I may have some pieces that are "classic Andy Lifschutz", but in general the world will see a great variety of work as I progress through life, interpreting through my own enriched experiences.' All the metals he uses are 100% reclaimed; the stones are either vintage or domestically sourced, and not from deep mines – an added value for jewelry that achieves a union of the organic, the enigmatic and the technical. As he notes, the impetus for his work has changed with time: 'My designs have evolved from the concept of "this would be a good seller and is interesting" to "this is something that I would like to explore and perfect".' We have found here nature's right hand.

www.andylifschutz.com

ANNDRA NEEN

The sculptural yet fashionably stylish qualities of Anndra Neen jewelry translate metal into a wearable art form. Born and raised in Mexico City, sisters Phoebe and Annette Stephens, jewelry makers extraordinaires, were brought up in a vibrant artistic community. Key to this was the influence of their grandmother, Annette, married to the composer Conlon Nancarrow, and her friends, who included legendary Mexican artists Diego Rivera, Frida Kahlo and José Clemente Orozco, to name but a few. Spiritually and artistically bolstered by this rich heritage (Annette Nancarrow was herself a jewelry designer as well as a painter and sculptor),

the siblings launched Anndra Neen in 2009, following a trip to Japan. Their creative symbiosis delivers aesthetically pitch-perfect metallic renditions. 'Our design process is really organic. We throw ideas back and forth. One of us will start a sketch and the other will finish it. We then produce the sample, which we wear to feel how it works on the body,' they explain. Diverse and daring, yet classic in essence, their creations are obvious tributes to antique design blueprints. The duo carry out a purposeful immersion in major cultural civilizations to retrieve craft techniques and concoct contemporary interpretations. 'We love working with silver, and some of our favourite materials are rough-cut black diamonds and rose gold,' they note. 'As for our dream project, it would be to work with Viennese master silversmiths.' The *Cage* series typifies their style: the structural frame of each piece is deceptively minimalist, yet majestic enough to confer plenty of graphic elegance and to make onlookers shed envious glances at the Anndra Neen wearer. Conformity is no longer an option.

http://anndraneen.com

OPPOSITE ABOVE LEFT 'Coral Reef' necklace of Alpaca silver, with ribbon.

OPPOSITE ABOVE CENTRE 'Large Cage' cuff of Alpaca silver and brass.

OPPOSITE ABOVE RIGHT 'Peak' ring of Alpaca silver and brass.

OPPOSITE BELOW It all starts with a sketch: musing over an 'Oval Open Cage' clutch, while wearing a 'Cone Bangle' cuff.

CLOCKWISE FROM ABOVE

'Cage' choker of Alpaca silver and brass.

'V' choker of Alpaca silver and brass.

'Vertical Hammered' ring of Alpaca silver and brass.

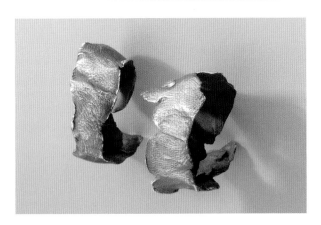

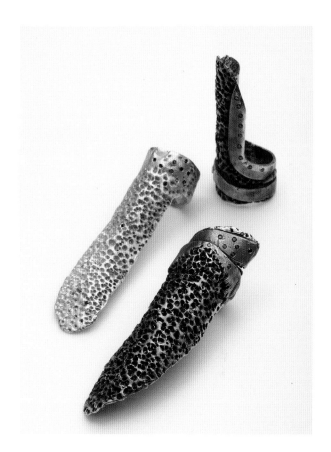

DARCY MIRO

What impresses most is the way in which Darcy Miro's creations resemble organic shields – beautiful, abstract, metal wraps that are products of the intense vision of a forward-thinker. Brooklyn-based Darcy is a free-spirited artist, who studied the orthodoxy and rules of jewelry and metalsmithing at college. She learned the importance of being technically precise, of measuring everything perfectly and not improvising. But after graduating she did a complete about-turn, making everything organically. 'I found a way to work naturally with the metal, especially silver,' she says. 'I have always made things. There was never any question as to what I would do. The only question was what medium I would obsess over enough to explore for life.' As she recalls: 'I found metal and I love the science of it, the metallurgy. It's so strong and resilient. It has a memory. It's forgiving. It also has a mind of its own and can become anything.' Darcy sees herself as a visionary who pursues her ideas relentlessly and is always willing to push the envelope to make new discoveries – so much so that she will try anything at least once. 'I haven't closed any doors, nor do I operate within boundaries or in boxes. I straddle every distinct line that has been established,' she asserts. This spectacular openness to the possibilities of her material and craft is underlined by the fact that she is equally at ease sculpting monumental structures as making jewelry, thereby addressing both the functional and purely aesthetic realms of her art. But all the while she employs her wizardry systematically to charge her metal with an almost feline grace. Metal has been tamed.

www.darcymiro.com

GLAUCO CAMBI

When jewelry meets sculpture, it transcends fashion and takes on the infinite perspectives of 3D. Glauco Cambi, Italian artisan and artist (he is also a painter and sculptor), realized that the human body was the perfect display stand for small-scale sculptures. 'In my jewel-objects, shapes are endlessly chased,' he relates, 'but the greatest pleasure lies in their changeable nature, in watching them move with the body that is wearing them.' Glauco has to have a clear idea before he begins his manual work; only then does he start to think about colours, stones and metals. He has a particular affinity for stones that change with the light and that contain peculiar inclusions, and he enjoys unstable metals that react and oxidize, such as silver, bronze, copper and, more recently, titanium. He also enjoys experimenting with the *mokume-gane* metalworking technique. The methods he favours – knotting, squeezing, nailing, scratching – become integral parts of the final creation. 'Mutability, the ways in which perception can be altered, the mobility of the mechanical and the instability of the visible form are the basic stylistic elements of my work,' he explains. Take the *attraction* project, which attests to his ingenuity and creative drive: the pieces in this series contain invisible micro-magnets that constantly attract and repel one another, making the forms seem temporarily frozen in movement. 'Nothing is ever left to an easy solution,' he says. 'I love my work when I am not falling into some self-referential trap, when my hands don't take advantage of the freedom they have, when they are thinking. In those moments, I own what I do.' And we are in awe.

www.glaucocambi.it

CLOCKWISE FROM LEFT

'Magnetic Attraction' earrings in bronze, yellow gold and agate (the gold spheres are suspended).

Ring of yellow gold, patinated bronze, positive quartz and diamonds, *Knots* series.

One-of-a-kind ring in patinated bronze, yellow gold and chlorite quartz.

'Nero' ring of ebony, yellow gold, hessonite and diamonds.

'3 Cubes' ring of yellow gold, bronze and quartz cubes, *Stretch* series.

TOP LEFT 'Mixed' charm bracelet of sterling silver, 24kt gold over bronze charms and glass pearl drop detail.

ABOVE LEFT 'Gold Bud' earrings, buds in 24kt gold over bronze with freshwater pearls, 14kt gold-filled wire ear hooks; 'Gold Lace Disc' necklace of 24kt gold over bronze, 14kt gold-filled chain; and 'Gold Caviar' necklace, cap in 24kt gold over bronze, resin set with freshwater pearls, rose quartz stone, fibre-optic beads, 14kt gold-filled chain.

TOP RIGHT 'Lace Drop' earrings of sterling silver discs and chain, woven freshwater pearls.

ABOVE RIGHT 'Sea Drift' ring of sterling silver and freshwater pearls woven on 14kt gold-filled wire.

OPPOSITE ABOVE 'Sea Star' collar necklace of sterling silver with freshwater pearl.

OPPOSITE BELOW Making the most of nature's patterns: an old botanical book for inspiration, the sketches that derive from it and one wax result.

LOUISE DOUGLAS

Louise Douglas's workshop, surrounded by mountains and the sound of birdsong, sits in the arty seaside town of Nelson, New Zealand. The immediacy of nature and the ocean seems entwined in Louise's creative DNA. 'Designing a new species of underwater plantlife, something a mermaid would wear, is in my creative sights,' she confides. She started designing and selling to fashion stores throughout New Zealand at the age of 18. Three years later she moved to New York, designing for large fashion jewelry houses and learning the ropes of the business, before eventually returning home. 'I design for the person I believe is my customer. She is a woman that likes unique keepsakes, jewelry that relates to a free and organic sensibility. I am also convinced that my creations have a certain femininity that speaks to a woman's desire to feel beautiful. If I sense it when I try on a piece, it will work,' she reflects. Louise scouts plants, organic textures, scientific drawings, anything biological that may produce the spark that will form the basis of a collection. 'I've always been inspired by the intricacies of the natural world. I love art and fashion, too, but the truth is that what I am always most inspired by stems from nature,' she says. Pearls, cherished for their umpteen dazzling hues, are married with chiselled naturalistic mineral renditions, which instantly soften the raw arabesques, branches or rock surfaces of silver and gold. Louise's work is a lyrical ode to nature that preserves its perfect imperfections and ensures that all the details are in place: a pretty ear hook, perhaps, or a well-curved clasp. This exquisite femininity radiates way beyond Down Under.

www.louisedouglas.com

RIGHT Pamela Love's inspiration den: striking illustrations and cultural memorabilia.

BELOW 'Double Snake' rings of silver with champagne diamonds and emeralds, and 14kt gold with diamonds and rubies.

PAMELA LOVE

The force be with you. Gleaming crystals shoot out of a sculptural cuff; porcupine quills extend defiantly from a low-strung chain; jagged gems adorn a talismanic ring. The striking creations of New York designer Pamela Love are the ultimate sensual armour for alpha females and males. Composed of a variety of materials, from brass and leather to 14kt gold and precious stones, they evoke a futuristic warrior tribe, yet hold an otherworldly charm. This paradox surely derives from the fact that Pamela's work forays indiscriminately into fine and costume jewelry, employing an artful balance of skilled techniques (working with metals and chemicals) and quixotic additions (flourishes and embellishments). Her creations are always spot on trend, but are never mere fads. Pamela majored in film production at New York University, then worked as artist Francesco Clemente's painting assistant and as an art director and stylist for photo shoots, music videos and films. 'When I was working as a stylist,' she recalls, 'I often struggled to find the kinds of pieces I envisioned for a specific look, so I just started making my own. I've always been fascinated by the creative process, from film to clothing to anything that involves making something whole out of disparate parts. Jewelry is the ultimate construction project.' Her first collection debuted in 2008 and has gone from strength to strength, partly thanks to some impressive collaborations – Marchesa, Twenty8 Twelve, MAC, Zac Posen, Opening Ceremony, Spike Jonze and HBO's *True Blood* among them. With the support of a dedicated in-house team, each piece of jewelry in the line receives personal attention from start to finish. Every new collection is exciting and different, all the while maintaining the key traits that tie it to Pamela's previous work. These are pieces that will last for a lifetime, and beyond.

www.pamelalovenyc.com

BELOW 'Ridge' cuff in bronze.

CENTRE 'Tribal Spike' cuffs in antique silver and antique bronze.

RIGHT 'Tribal Spike' necklace in antique silver with quartz crystal.

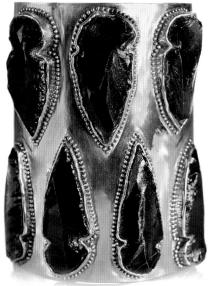

ABOVE 'Arrowhead' rings in sterling silver with obsidian, flint and quartz stones.

LEFT 'Arrowhead' cuff in bronze with obsidian stones.

CLOCKWISE FROM RIGHT

'Crystal Crescent' necklace in gold and green.

'Quartz' crystal cuff in bronze.

'Navarro' ring in gold with rubies.

'Crystal Block' cuff in bronze and green.

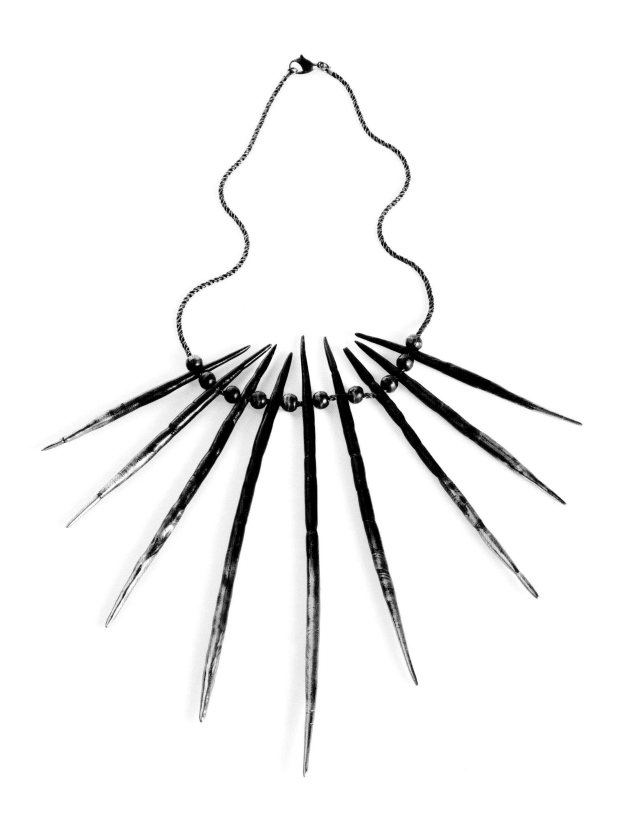

ABOVE 'Porcupine Needle' necklace in bronze.

BELOW AND RIGHT Rings in sterling silver,
Sensum Ring series.

ABOVE 'Elvish Twine' ring of sterling silver
and rough aquamarine.

LEFT 'Elvish Haunted Willow' ring of sterling
silver and rough citrine.

REDSOFA BY JOANNA SZKIELA

What more fitting guide could we hope for than a self-confessed 'loner, non-conformist, corporate dropout' metalsmith from Montreal to take us on a creative journey through uncharted territories, where metal is the reigning deity? RedSofa is Joanna Szkiela's jewelry line for men and women. Her predilection for dark-hewn sterling silver and uncut stones is a direct homage to the sculptural, edgy side of metalsmithing. Joanna recalls being 'intrigued and conquered' the moment she soldered her first silver band: 'I was terrified of the torch and having to work with fire, so making it happen left such a powerful impression of happiness and

accomplishment. I realized how it suddenly opened the door to a place where anything I wanted became possible.' Her work is deeply ingrained with organic references. 'Metals, whether silver or gold, are definitely my favourites. They are like a blank canvas, or almost like a clay that I can model to whatever shape I want. I use stones, wood, natural pearls and other found objects to highlight the qualities of metal.' The extraordinary malleability of silver and gold means Joanna can skydive from a magical alchemical world: in some pieces, burgeoning circles ripple outwards, as if towed by vital motion; in others, metals encase rough stones, like gatekeepers sheltering a sacred fire; in still other, perhaps more confounding examples, it is almost possible to visualize the movement of slender tentacles. 'I am a passionate observer and I am fascinated by nature and human nature,' confides Joanna. 'I tend to gravitate towards decidedly feral forms. The more I explore an idea, the more inspired I become to create new pieces. It seems as if work evolves from work.' Long may she continue to show us the way.

http://gotoredsofa.com

'Echelon' earrings in brass.

Pitch-perfect lightness, balance and proportion, found in both Hanna Sandin's workspace and creations.

'Flat Peak' bracelet in brass.

'Dangler' necklace in brass.

'Stack' and 'Semaphore' necklaces in brass.

'Echelon Sliding' and 'Echelon Tennis' bracelets and an 'Echelon Double' ring, all in brass.

'Semaphore', 'Stack' and 'Openface' bracelets and a 'Hi-Top' ring, all in brass.

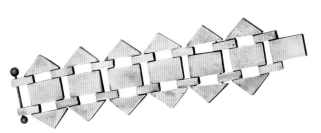

SAMMA

'Primitive meets the mechanical age' is how Hanna Sandin describes the creative style behind her jewelry label SAMMA (Swedish for 'same'). On the surface, her work is beautifully simple, linear and humble. But it is also shaped by an immensely skilful human hand that is able to manipulate base metal into surrendering its true self. 'My line eschews looking like "fine" jewelry. It is crude by choice; brash but somehow, I hope, elegant as well.' SAMMA grew out of Hanna's work as a sculptor – a clue as to why her pieces exhibit such tactile functionality. It all started with the 'Triangle' necklace. 'I now try to hang on to the ease of that first piece,' Hanna reflects. 'You really couldn't add anything to it or take anything away.' Simple, triangular beads on a cotton rope, with a double knot that slides, spelled instant success. 'I conceptualize my pieces in families that are defined by forms and how things fit together, and the process by which individual components are made. There is a strict visual language composed of modular parts that can fit together or be assembled in a multitude of ways – bundling, weaving, small bricks, big bricks,' she explains. 'But uniformity is always broken by hints that the work is handmade. Even though I reference machined metal, everything is cast and polished individually, so that the little irregularities lend warmth to an otherwise almost rigid vocabulary.' Inspired by, among others, Naum Slutzky and Art Smith, as well as the Bauhaus design style and mass-produced Art Deco jewelry of Jakob Bengel, Hanna defers to primary forms. This is 'anti-statement' jewelry at its finest, defined not by ostentatious wealth but by a pared-down, formalistic sensibility.

http://sammasamma.com

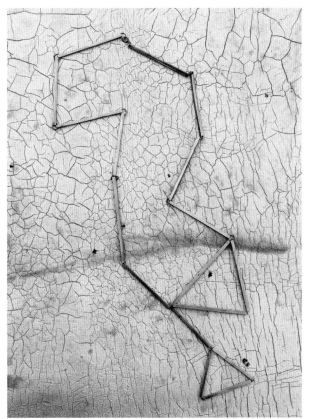

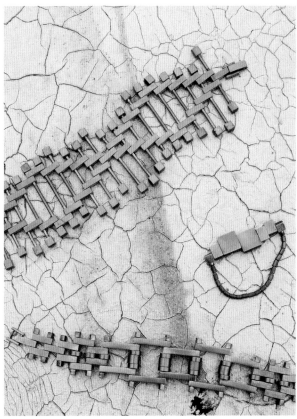

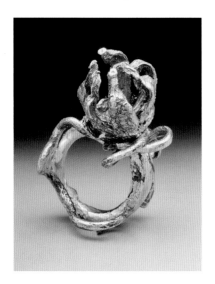

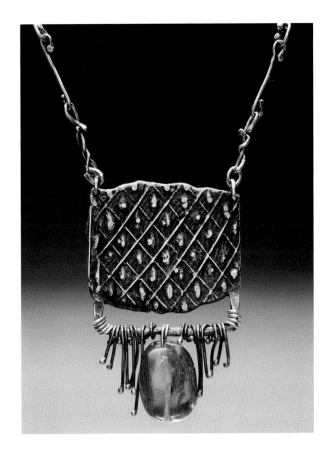

STACY HOPKINS

One could be forgiven for thinking that illuminati are behind these astounding, elemental, fossil-like creations. Exuding the sacred rawness of shamanistic treasures, each piece emulates a 'rite of passage' token from the occult workshop of a medieval blacksmith – a reminder of forces larger than ourselves. These are artifacts worthy of a natural history museum, and they result from the creator's scientific approach. Decay and imperfection, key stages in the natural lifecycle, are immortalized in bronze, gold or silver casts. The alchemist? None other than the American designer/activist/inspiration Stacy Hopkins. A former biologist, Stacy has channelled her interest in the sciences through artistic and political pursuits. 'Metal can take on some amazingly different identities, from hardcore to refined, primal to futuristic. There is an archaic essence to working with metal and shaping it through heat and mechanical means. It catalyzes my creativity,' she says. 'Sometimes my work takes me in its own direction and I learn a lot from mistakes and spontaneity. There is much to be gained from not over-controlling material.' Rare flora and endangered species are at the centre of her creative preoccupations; so too a heightened environmental consciousness. 'I don't know what it will take to protect the planet when we're up against such bulldozing greed,' she says, 'but I like to voice this desire through my work, which re-establishes our personal and inherent relationship with nature.' A percentage of the profits from her *Endangered – Costa Rica* collection is donated to land conservation and the protection of endangered species. Bypassing the modern impulse to churn out cheap, meaningless products, Stacy sculpts pieces with an integrity that elevates the soul.

www.stacy-hopkins-design.com

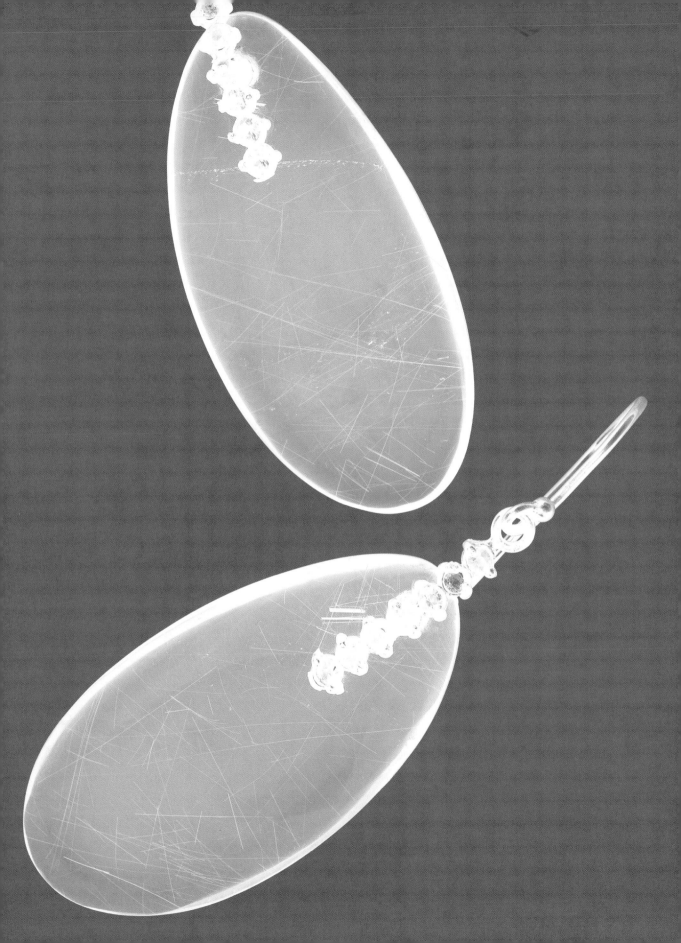

THE
NEO-CLASSICS

Modern creations that will become timeless heirlooms.
Grace and elegance in unconventional goldsmithing.

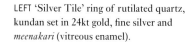

LEFT 'Silver Tile' ring of rutilated quartz, kundan set in 24kt gold, fine silver and *meenakari* (vitreous enamel).

BELOW LEFT 'Silk Route Tile' ring of lemon quartz, baguette peridots, kundan set in 24kt gold, 22kt gold and *meenakari*.

BELOW RIGHT 'Silver Tile' ring of peridot, kundan set in 24kt gold, fine silver and *meenakari*.

BOTTOM Alice Cicolini's design table with hand-carved ebony models and sketchbooks.

ALICE CICOLINI

At the Mehrangarh Fort in Jodhpur, Alice Cicolini's attention is caught by a jewelry box that would once have belonged to a member of the Indian royal family. She starts to imagine what kind of jewels it might have contained, and she wonders how she can create a collection that will celebrate India's craft and ritual traditions but in a contemporary way. This was the experience that sparked Alice's idea for a unique jewelry label. After over a decade curating exhibitions on fashion and contemporary design, and many years working with product designer Tom Dixon, Alice graduated with an MA in jewelry design from Central St Martin's in London in 2009. 'Jewelry feels like the perfect environment for me,' she remarks, 'situated somewhere between fashion, art and craftsmanship; a place where my knowledge and experience contribute to what I do. This fluidity, or refusal of the possibility of fixed definition, also makes jewelry an interesting place for someone who likes to tell stories. And I love colour, which jewelry indulges in abundance.' Above all, Alice's approach helps to ensure the survival of ancient craft traditions. 'The sacred architecture and patterns of the Silk Route were the inspiration for my first collection,' she notes, recognizing how her work as a curator has informed her style. 'Finding the connections and resonances between

ideas and objects continues to inspire my design.' She works with Indian masters from Jaipur who possess unique craft techniques, including *meenakari*, the art of decorating metal by enamelling. This collaboration, combined with her skilful enrichment of noble materials such as ebony, gemstones and gold, means that she is able to create timeless, one-of-a-kind pieces that have great poetic and cultural resonance. Her elegant, sensual creations are jewelry's contribution to modern antiquity.

www.alicecicolini.com

'Temple Lotus' earrings of hand-carved ebony, 18kt gold and diamonds.

'Silk Route Meena' pendant necklace of 22kt gold, *meenakari*, hand-carved ebony, 18kt gold beads and Indian hand-faceted ruby beads.

'Temple Lemon' ring of lemon quartz, kundan set in 24kt gold, hand-carved ebony and 18kt gold.

BELOW 'Origine' earrings in 18kt yellow gold.

RIGHT 'Gangue' necklace of 18kt yellow gold
and multicoloured gems.

BELOW RIGHT 'Organique' ring of 18kt yellow gold and white diamonds.

FAR RIGHT 'Nymphea' ring of 18kt yellow gold and smoky quartz.

BOTTOM Faithful to Aude Lechère's passion for pâtisserie: appetizingly colourful sketches for the *Macarons* collection.

AUDE LECHÈRE

Flaming multicoloured cabochons, as deliciously appealing as sugar-coated toppings, sit upon a papal ring as scrumptious as golden, freshly whipped cream. It is no surprise that pâtisserie-making is also one of designer Aude Lechère's passions. At the heart of her jewelry can be found sensory indulgence and bravura artistry. 'A collection always starts with the design of the ring,' she explains. 'The other pieces in the collection then flow organically. I couldn't live without a ring; it's the centrepiece of jewelry that one often cherishes most.' The timeless, sensual appeal of Aude's creations is the result of extraordinary technical prowess with an emotive pull (proportions are meticulously conceptualized; facets and purposeful irregularities encourage close scrutiny). A sense of exuberance is skilfully tamed by Aude's obsession with finding the right balance between the final piece and the way it sits on the body. She explains that her first collection, *Pépite*, heralded a signature style: 'I worked gold nuggets by faceting them unevenly, and this is a technique I've been using ever since. As for the selection of gems, I keep it open. It has to be love at first sight, and I always look for unconventional combinations.' Her radiant, head-turning creations did not languish in obscurity for long – the luxury department store Barneys New York placed an order soon after detecting media interest in the upcoming designer. The crafted medieval-style roughness of her pieces, the deceptive fragility, is combined with a delight in asymmetry, pale-coloured precious gems and intensely hued tiger's eyes and moonstones. 'I like the fact that jewels should wait for their owner,' she whispers. The cognoscenti are already standing in line.

www.aude-lechere.com

'Maracas' ring of 18kt yellow gold and citrine.

'Mie de Pain' cuff of 18kt yellow gold.

'Planète' cuff of 18kt yellow gold and
multicoloured cabochon gems.

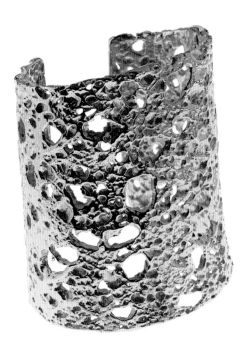

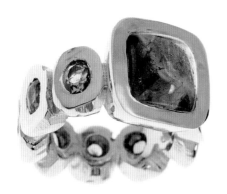

'Sissi' ring of 18kt yellow gold, green tourmaline and pink sapphire.

'Impératrice' ring of 18kt yellow gold, amethyst and grey moonstone cabochons.

'Dentelle' ring of 18kt yellow gold and lemon quartz.

'Queen II' ring of 18kt yellow gold, pink quartz and peridot.

BELOW Earrings of 21kt gold, opal enamel and South Sea pearls.

RIGHT Colourful, warm and bright: Eva's workshop reflects the qualities of her creations.

BOTTOM Rings of 21kt gold and rubies; sterling silver, 21kt gold and peridot; and 18kt white gold and aquamarine.

OPPOSITE ABOVE Necklace of 21kt gold and aquamarine beads.

OPPOSITE BELOW LEFT Bracelet of 21kt solid gold, kunzite beads and opal enamel.

OPPOSITE BELOW RIGHT Earrings of 21kt gold, opal enamel and cultured pearls.

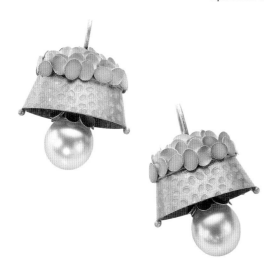

EVA STEINBERG

Byzantine sophistication and sweet sherbert colours convey a sense of springtime – jewelry's answer to a soothing balm. Scalloped, leaf- and heart-shaped enamel ornaments nestle tiny pearls like delicate stigma on exquisite waterlily earrings; a gold-beaded necklace, interspersed with faceted gems, radiates rays of light like the feathers of a mythical bird. German goldsmith Eva Steinberg invents jewelry that unlocks our yearning for harmony and wellbeing. 'I'm always coming up with new projects. They form as dream visions and keep my passion burning,' she confides. 'The progress I see in my work consists of the combination of ever more techniques, more variations in colour and more vitality being injected into each creation.' Eva has a love for the glowing warmth of gold, the silky lustre of pearls, the weightlessness and transparency of amber, and the multiple colorations of enamel. She creates highly constructed and layered jewels that nevertheless evoke tremendous lightness. Her work is, in short, a complex and artful jigsaw. 'I want my jewelry to act as a counterbalance to the suffering that is everywhere in the world, including my own personal suffering. I want to create something beautiful to lull the soul and attract the eye of the viewer,' she muses. 'I work with precious materials that have historical associations with

symbolism and myth. It's exciting for me to be able to contribute to the human impulse to be adorned, and that's why I assemble these materials in the most harmonious compositions possible.' Eva's art is an ode to femininity that exudes a sense of blissful respite. In fact, her jewelry should probably be prescribed daily.

www.eva-steinberg.de

BELOW 'Tahitian Sea Anemone' ring of Tahitian pearl surrounded by multicoloured sapphires and diamonds set in 18kt gold, *The South Sea* collection.

LEFT 'Pearl Reef' pendant necklace of diamonds and pearls set in 18kt white gold, South Sea pearl drop, *The South Sea* collection.

ABOVE RIGHT 'Anemone' bangle of pink and yellow sapphires set in 18kt white gold with a marquise diamond, *The South Sea* collection.

ABOVE 'Tahitian Sea Anemone' earrings of tourmaline set in 18kt gold, surrounded by diamonds and sapphires with Tahitian pearl, *The South Sea* collection.

BELOW 'Coral' earrings of mandarin,
pink and yellow sapphires set in 18kt gold,
The South Sea collection.

RIGHT Ephemera and memorabilia for
inspiration compose a glam-chic décor.

BELOW RIGHT Tools of the trade: a saw
for piercing and shaping metal, and a flex
shaft for sculpting and polishing.

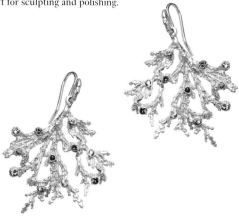

KIMBERLIN BROWN

Kimberlin Brown has introduced a bold new vocabulary into the world of jewelry design, in which organic growth forms the basis of creativity. What inspires Kimberlin's precious compositions is the pure, natural beauty of underwater nirvanas – and she scouts these rich hunting grounds for treasure. 'I grew up in a beach town in Connecticut called Greenwich. My childhood was peaceful and always near the water, which explains why I am still now most at peace by the sea,' she notes. Her fascination with the ocean inspired her favourite collection to date – *The South Sea* collection. Enthralled by the lustre and colour of Tahitian pearls, Kimberlin celebrates their luminosity by nestling them regally in miniature coral reefs that are cast in 18kt white or yellow gold. Diamonds, tourmalines and multicoloured sapphires inject vital shimmering accents. Kimberlin is currently working on 'a big, ornate cuff that will look as if Poseidon had it made for his Sea Goddess Queen' – another enchanting ambassador from the ocean depths. This body of work, stimulated by, but not derived from, ocean resources, has led Kimberlin into partnership with the ocean-conservation group Sea Web and the 'Too Precious to Wear' campaign. 'Alongside Frank Gehry and Paloma Picasso, as well as environmentalist film-maker Céline Cousteau,

I am helping to spread awareness about the critical situation our oceans are facing,' she says. Another prime example of the dedication and integrity that makes owning and wearing a piece by Kimberlin Brown all the more meaningful a privilege.

http://kimberlinbrownjewelry.com

LAURENT GANDINI

Recognizing the value of your cultural heritage is one thing; embarking on a mission to revisit its popular jewelry traditions, in particular the peasant tradition, is quite another. Milan-based jeweler Laurent Gandini, in interpreting rural and folkloric themes, produces unique pieces that are notable for their extreme femininity and gentility. He is the mastermind behind a sumptuous collection of lace-like chandelier earrings, signet rings and other trinkets that could pass for metal embroidery. He explains the stages involved in his working process: 'I start by researching patterns or architectural decorations from Italian popular traditions. When

something inspires me, I draw until I reach the "perfect" form. Then I model the wax or I work directly on the silver plate, cutting and modelling all the individual elements that compose the earring or the necklace.' Laurent began making jewelry in 1990, and his first commission was for Missoni. Since 1999 he has divided his time between running his own business and overseeing the silver accessory collections for the Italian fashion house Costume National. He chooses to work with comparatively 'low' precious materials, such as 9kt rose gold (often used in jewelry in the Italian countryside at the beginning of the twentieth century), and he revels in developing a slightly grandiose modern interpretation of traditional Italian style. But he declares, 'I am the antithesis of a designer. I have been creating for twenty years and I have never looked into the future for concepts. My design method hasn't really changed since I began.' The underlying themes of his work include the cult of Catholic saints, popular superstition and folk rites, but these aspects inform rather than dominate the final execution to ensure that timelessness and sensuality remain the hallmarks of Laurent Gandini's art.

www.laurentgandini.com

'Big Chandelier' earrings in 9kt rose gold
and grey labradorite.

'Ex-Voto' earrings in 9kt rose gold.

'Sigillo' rings in silver with torsade-decorated,
rose gold bezels and rock crystal, which acts like
a magnifying glass for hidden encased patterns.

BELOW 'Double Touch' ring of 18kt yellow gold and pearl, *Touch* collection.

RIGHT 'Light' bracelet of 18kt yellow gold and pearls, *Touch* collection.

BOTTOM 'Gomitoli' necklace of 18kt yellow gold and small pearls, *Gomitoli* collection.

BELOW 'Forme' earrings of 18kt yellow
gold and pearl, *Poligoni* collection.

RIGHT 'Net' bracelet of 18kt yellow gold
and small pearls, *Knot* collection.

BELOW RIGHT 'Sewing' black diamonds,
threaded on a wire, into the yellow gold
ring of a piece from the *Frame* collection.

LIA DI GREGORIO

In Lia di Gregorio's work, geometrical simplicity is offset
by unexpected elements that challenge our perceptions:
some gems are concealed, others float as if defying gravity.
It is poetry with an edge, science with grace. For more than
twenty-five years the Italian jewelry designer has been pushing the boundaries of what is possible by revolutionizing
the rules of proportion and confounding the fundamental
principles of assembly. Passionate about representational
art and architecture, Lia moves in the most influential art
circles in Italy. It is here that she shares, learns and gets
inspired. 'I brainstorm and sketch,' she enthuses. 'When an
idea comes, I sample with various materials, such as paper,
brass and copper. Once the project takes shape, I do a final
drawing that incorporates all the details for the construction of the piece.' She has a predilection for gold, diamonds
and pearls, which, apart from their decorative role, play
an integral part in her ingenious constructions. 'I like the
neutral colour of pearls; and rubies and black diamonds for
the striking simplicity of the red and black,' she declares.
Borrowing techniques that are not traditionally associated
with jewelry making, she uses gold wires as if they were silk
threads to embroider as well as crochet gems onto the frame
of her pieces. She explores, melts, solders and chisels ... and

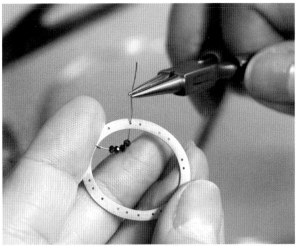

assumes complete mastery over the behaviour of the metal.
The result? Unfussy compositions that have great harmony
and equilibrium, and that bring gentleness. The purity of the
lines is a testimony to modernity, yet the sculptural forms
awaken our senses. This is jewelry that is so much more than
the sum of its parts.

www.liadigregorio.com

MARGERY HIRSCHEY

'A woman wearing all black and sandals, with her hair swept up in a French twist, black eyeliner, drinking an espresso in a smoky coffee shop while reading poetry. A beatnik from those old French movies from the early sixties.' This is how Margery Hirschey imagines her muse. Her graceful creations ooze versatile chic – think exquisitely hued gems mounted on recycled gold, in the manner of antique jewels. 'I love pure gold. I can see why ancient cultures associated it with the glow of the sun,' she remarks. 'I also love the colours of old things, because they only had natural dyes, or because things have faded over time. To me those colours are an endless source of inspiration.' An intuitive artisan and artist, Margery revels in replicating the human-charged aspect of historic pieces. She preserves the raw brilliance of gold and opts exclusively for rare stones with natural inclusions and eloquent imperfections. 'I have some earrings that have beautiful misshapen pearls on the bottom. The pearls have these gorgeous soft colours that I was told were actually caused by pollution in the water. Go figure!' she laughs. It must be her upbringing, with hours spent exploring museums, that accounts for the fact that her work is so attuned to a sense of permanence and timelessness. But each of her pieces is also veiled with a modern

warmth – stones in a harmonious and contemporary colour spectrum; cuts creating an organic yet graphic balance. 'The mere fact that I can actually make a piece of jewelry enthrals me,' she exclaims. 'Let's face it, women love jewelry.' They do, and they most certainly love Margery's.

www.margeryhirschey.com

OPPOSITE ABOVE LEFT Earrings of 22kt gold, oxidized sterling silver, diamond and tourmaline.

OPPOSITE ABOVE RIGHT Margery Hirschey marking out an outline to saw through a sheet of gold.

OPPOSITE BELOW Ring of 22kt gold, boulder opal and diamond.

CLOCKWISE FROM TOP

Necklace of 18kt gold, green tourmaline, rose-cut diamond and sapphire.

Earrings of 22kt gold, blackened sterling silver, tourmalines and spinel.

Earrings of 22kt gold, oxidized sterling silver, moonstone and boulder opal.

CLOCKWISE FROM LEFT

'Tube and Labradorite' necklace of vermeil gold and labradorite.

'Playing Cats' bangle of vermeil gold and chrome tourmalines.

'Triangles with Diamond' ring of 18kt gold with rose-cut diamond macle.

BELOW 'Large Quartz' ring of sterling silver and rose-cut rutilated quartz.

RIGHT 'Birds with Pearls' earrings of vermeil gold and AAA-quality freshwater pearls.

BOTTOM Vito the cat rummaging through large aqua stones, or is he helping his owner choose which ones will befit the final 'Large Aqua' ring?

NATALIE FRIGO

Natalie Frigo's overriding ambition is to spearhead a movement establishing sustainable practices in jewelry. Supporting local economies, assuring fair pay to mining communities, using recycled metals and conflict-free and fair-trade stones – these are the issues close to her heart. 'On average, the mining of an ounce of gold or silver creates thirty tons of waste. One common practice is to dump excavated materials into giant pools, then douse the area with sodium cyanide, leaching out any precious metals, with all its destructive consequences,' she explains. 'Recycled metal and newly mined metal are indistinguishable, so the choice is an easy one.' With this ethos in mind, Natalie revisits ancient cultures – mostly Egyptian and Etruscan – by sculpting jewelry that acts as a visual metaphor for modern antiquities. 'I especially love the presence of a craftsperson's hand in ancient jewelry,' she notes. 'My pieces used to be smoother and rounder, but now I really enjoy having a lot of angular textures and scratches on the surface of my work, paired with chunky, irregularly shaped stones.' Pearls and natural, uncut diamonds illuminate curvaceous frames; little cats and birds punctuate chiselled gold trinkets. 'I love to work in minute detail. It's inherent in my creative process: the smaller the detail, the better. I can work intensely on a piece for hours at a time and not lose interest,' she confides. Ancient Chinese artifacts found in the Atlantic, near the Bahamas, have recently fired her imagination, though 'there's some debate as to whether these organically shaped objects are anchors or just naturally formed stones'. Like a treasure hunter, Natalie trawls through the past, transforming its mysteries into highly crafted tokens with solid ethical guarantees. We now know where to turn.

http://bynataliefrigo.com

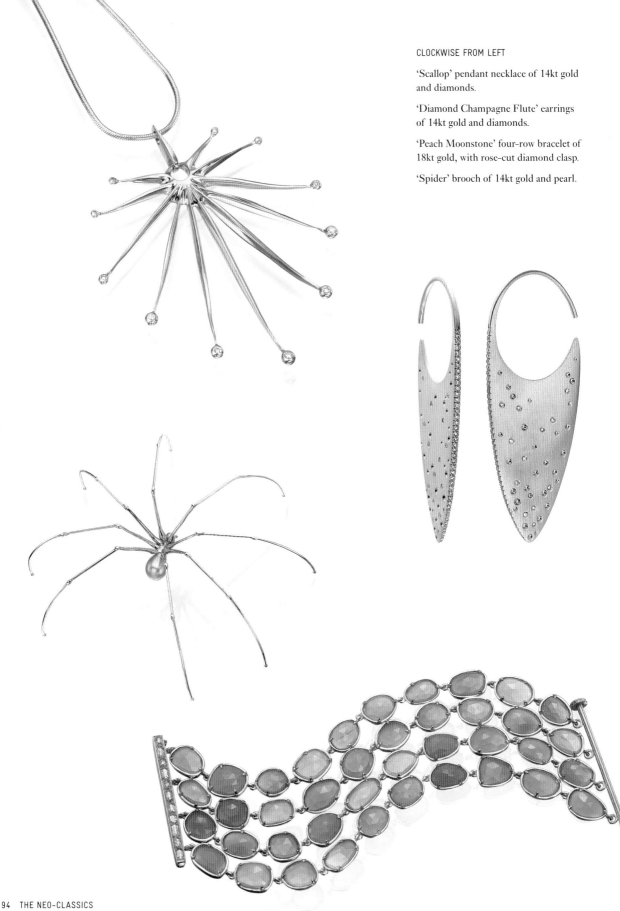

'Scallop' pendant necklace of 14kt gold and diamonds.

'Diamond Champagne Flute' earrings of 14kt gold and diamonds.

'Peach Moonstone' four-row bracelet of 18kt gold, with rose-cut diamond clasp.

'Spider' brooch of 14kt gold and pearl.

NICOLE LANDAW

Peach moonstones sway delicately within the four strands of
an 18kt gold bracelet; a rutilated quartz rests regally between
the clean arches of a cuff; a soft pink pearl completes the body
of an impossibly delicate spider brooch. In each of these
pieces, serenity reigns supreme. Nicole Landaw's unique
talent is evident in her sublimely understated yet unmistakably feminine pieces. 'When first I discovered that I could
move metal to create expressive forms, I was captivated,'
she recalls. 'And that sense of possibility and enchantment
is still with me and calls me to the bench.' Nicole's favourite part of the crafting process is the critical middle stage,
when a piece's formal composition and relationship to the
semi-precious stones she custom-designs and cuts are carefully considered and formed. 'It's an incredibly exciting
time of discovery, creation and revision. If a brass band
marched through my studio during that time, I might not
even notice,' she laughs. Her singular, refined signature and
her bespoke service have landed her exciting collaborations
with fashion and costume designers, film and TV directors
… not to mention an ever-growing band of loyal customers,
some with extraordinary personal stories: 'A client recently
bought a pair of my earrings as a present to herself to wear
during her upcoming chemotherapy so that she would feel

beautiful and special. What higher compliment could I
receive?' Nicole muses. Congratulations to her for confer-
ring such an immaculate touch that every piece seems to
capture the elusive essence of timeless composure.

www.nicolelandaw.com

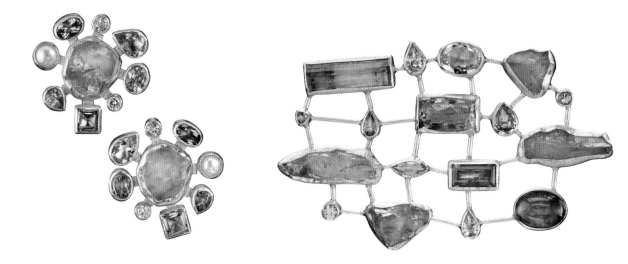

BELOW 'Blue Yellow Stars' earrings of
22kt/18kt gold, aquamarines, diamonds,
pearls and yellow sapphires.

BELOW RIGHT 'Seascape' brooch of 22kt/
18kt gold, aquamarines and yellow sapphires.

BOTTOM Flame in action: Petra Class soldering
with the use of a blowtorch.

PETRA CLASS

A cluster of irregular gemstones in myriad colours exudes a sense of grandeur and sets a new benchmark for eternal elegance. Looking at Petra Class's creations is a bit like stargazing. Like the pointers that map a constellation, gems of various cuts and shapes are mounted on gold grids in a homogenous display that eschews symmetry but embraces a distinctive palette. 'My approach to jewelry making,' German-born Petra has noted in an artist's statement, 'is informed foremost by the European tradition of applied art.' One has to look well back in time to discover when she decided that jewelry was her calling: 'It was after I dropped out of a circus school,' she admits. She trained as a silversmith and then spent several years constructing tableware. Today, based in San Francisco, Petra is above all a colour enthusiast, conceptualizing and then classifying her collections according to chromatic groupings. She reconciles kaleidoscopic brilliance with mathematics and the influence of structures in nature. Although she has no particular favourite gemstones – 'I am fickle; it changes frequently' – she is able to indicate recurring themes in her work: 'the rhythmical arrangements of several elements, repetition of similar forms or colours, and the unexpected contrasts of differently textured materials'. Her melodic compositions have the panache of creations by a Fauvist dilettante, pigments magnified and gems and stones highlighted. What would her dream project be? 'The child in me would like to make a tiara for the Snow Queen, or a necklace for Neptune's daughter,' she laughs. One can see perfectly well why Petra would be the ideal creator for such out-of-this-world commissions.

http://petraclass.net

CLOCKWISE FROM TOP

'Composition in Red and Yellow' necklace
of 22kt/18kt gold, rubies, tourmalines,
yellow sapphires, garnets, diamonds,
pearls and citrines.

'Red Mosaic' ring of 22kt/18kt gold
and red tourmalines.

'Blue Mosaic' ring of 22kt/18kt gold,
aquamarines and diamonds.

'Big Aquamarine' bracelet of 22kt/18kt gold
and rough aquamarines.

ABOVE 'Petite Aqua' necklace of aquamarine and 14kt gold.

RIGHT 'Grand Aqua' necklace of large aquamarine, diamonds and 14kt gold handmade chain.

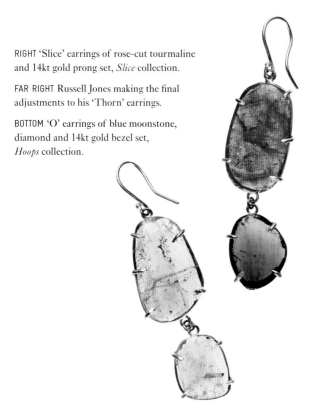

RUSSELL JONES

They are not what they seem ... or are they? Look beyond the spare and refined design lines and marvel at the fierce aesthetics that define Russell Jones's modern creations. In his *Facets* collection, the stones in the earrings may appear to be uniform and balanced but they have in fact been selected because they don't quite match. Imperfections are assets and construction is made visible: handmade prongs, bezels and rivets are considered prime elements in themselves. The result? Clean, high-end design. New York-based Russell graduated as an illustrator, but always had his sights set on mastering the art of metalsmithing. His career focused fully on jewelry in about 2005, but he has been making it since he was a teenager. His design process starts with the stones or beads he wants to showcase, 'then I draw until I'm happy. I may let a project sit for a while to make sure the idea is sound. Then I'll start making the piece. When moving from 2D to 3D, the design will change dramatically, yet get closer to the core idea.' He adds, 'I love the actual making of a piece more than the preparatory work, and I also really like to set stones.' Russell usually builds his work out of wire and sheet metal in silver, gold or, his favourite, palladium. He works closely with lapidaries, who hand-cut limited quantities of unusual precious or semi-precious stones especially for him

– most recently, new stones like brown sapphires, pyrite and meteorite. Even with his passion for craftsmanship and his forceful visionary drive, Russell ensures that 'spectacular' does not equal 'over the top'. How do people describe his work? 'Modern, well designed, unfussy. Stunning also ... a lot,' he says. When prompted to mention a dream project, he responds, 'A crown!' And a crown is what he deserves.

www.russelljonesjewelry.com

CLOCKWISE FROM LEFT

'Puddle' earrings of uniquely cut rutilated smoky quartz, black rhodium-plated silver, 18kt gold and pink sapphires, *Pavé* collection.

'Cluster' cuff of Honduran mahogany dyed black, rainbow moonstones and 14kt gold bezel settings.

'Moonstone' ring of carved onyx with orange moonstone, bezel set in 18kt gold countersunk, *Signet Ring* collection.

ABOVE 'Cross' earrings of uniquely cut carved
Indian turquoise, black rhodium-plated silver,
18kt gold, pink sapphires and diamonds,
Pavé collection.

RIGHT 'Cross' pin of rhodium-plated silver,
pink sapphires and diamonds, *Pavé* collection.

LEFT Earrings by Christian Streit in sterling silver, 24kt gold, copper and rock crystal.

BELOW Ring by Christian Streit in sterling silver, 18kt white gold, citrine and brilliant-cut 0.03ct diamond.

RIGHT Earrings by Silke Knetsch in sterling silver, 24kt gold, cabochon-cut carnelian and prasiolite.

BELOW Ring by Christian Streit in sterling silver, 24kt gold, onyx and 0.45ct diamond chips.

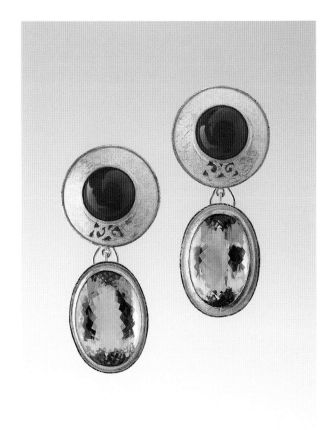

SILKE KNETSCH & CHRISTIAN STREIT

A multidimensional wizardry is at work in Silke Knetsch and Christian Streit's studio: baroque rings display painted edges that bring a delicate oriental touch to an architectural design; faceted, eclectically coloured gems shimmer within their comparatively austere setting; opulent earrings re-invent modern luxury with a royally decorative twist. The attention to detail is encapsulated best by the fact that each piece is as interesting from the back as it is from the front. Silke and Christian set up their workshop in Freiburg in 1997, after attending jewelry classes given by Ramón Puig Cuyás in Barcelona. Christian currently focuses on concepts such as asymmetric design using few stones. 'First I think thoroughly about what the piece should look like,' he explains, 'then I sketch it and work it in metal. The piece barely changes during the process.' Silke engages differently: 'I work less with design drawings and more with images I have in my head, which develop further in the design process. At all times, light and shadow play an important role as well.' These complementary approaches unite in a distinct sense of voluptuous luxuriance and sculptural elegance, enhanced by a strong commitment to sustainable entrepreneurship – use of fair-trade gold and silver, for example. The virtuoso technical skill on display lends a timeless quality to the jewelry. Silke and Christian seek to push the boundaries of their work ever further, while keeping their inimitable imprint on each piece. 'Jewelry is a medium that is limited by its size and wearability,' the pair note. 'Time and time again, we find it enticing to discover new possibilities within these borders and to defy them.' A glimpse here of their astute formula.

www.knetsch-streit.de / www.materia-prima.biz

Ring of 18kt yellow gold, rose-cut diamonds and raw diamond cubes, *Vintage* collection.

Stack of four 18kt yellow gold rings: white brilliant-cut diamonds; black fancy-cut diamond and white brilliant-cut diamonds; single eternity ring with raw diamond cubes; white pear-shaped fancy-cut diamond and white brilliant-cut diamonds, all *Bridal* collection.

Ring of 18kt yellow gold, natural coloured fancy-cut diamonds and white brilliant-cut diamonds, *Vintage* collection.

BELOW A bird's eye view inside Todd Reed's busy workshop/showroom in Colorado.

TODD REED

Todd Reed may be diamonds' most passionate right-hand man. So passionate, in fact, that he has been helping to reclaim what is truly precious about them – their unique natural inclusions and their mysteriously luminous yet opaque rawness. A self-taught goldsmith and jeweler, Todd was the first contemporary designer to use rough diamonds exclusively. He was the visionary trailblazer who challenged the status quo by introducing raw diamonds in a market committed to extreme faceting and illusory perfection under the 4Cs rule (carat, cut, colour and clarity). All this sprang from Todd's devotion to a belief that 'the most perfect cut is still

an uncut'. Years later, having received several major awards for his art, earned the loyalty of numerous like-minded collectors and customers, and established a shop/gallery/workshop in Boulder, Colorado, he is still going strong. He continues to advocate ethics and to celebrate the unaltered, natural form of diamonds through ultra-sumptuous jewelry that marries old-time allure with modern poise. 'My style is more emotional than business-driven. I've been designing since 1988 and I've gone through many changes,' he reflects. 'I think the most important change is learning to use restraint in design – not putting too many elements into one work. I like jewelry that is edgy and beautiful, unique and masterfully fabricated. It also comes to me as a "feeling" … it could be an energetic thing.' Scores of jewelers have jumped on the bandwagon by introducing rough diamonds into their collections; what was once summarily dismissed is now highly revered. So it's back to basics, just as nature and Todd Reed intended.

www.toddreed.com

CLOCKWISE FROM RIGHT

Necklace of 18kt yellow gold, natural rose-cut diamonds and raw diamond cubes, *Vintage* collection.

Pin brooch of 18kt yellow gold, silver, rose-cut diamonds, brilliant-cut diamonds and raw diamond cubes, *Vintage* collection.

Armband of 18kt yellow gold, natural coloured rose-cut diamonds and raw diamond cubes, *Vintage* collection.

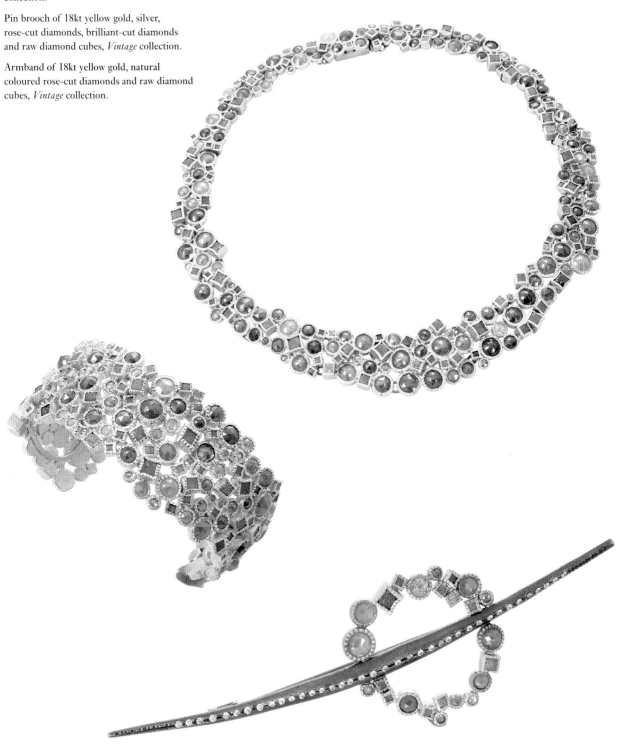

COOL LUXURY

Reject excess and cherish contemporary
keepsakes that befit a casual chic attitude.
You own it, and you know it.

LEFT 'sr-13' multi-strand bracelet in rose vermeil, *Silver Rocket* collection.

BELOW 'ada-10' bracelet in solid sterling silver, *Adding and* collection.

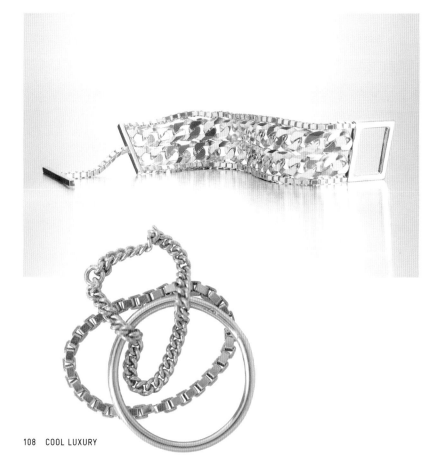

ABOVE LEFT 'ch-08' bracelet in solid sterling silver, *Charles* collection.

ABOVE 'ch-11' knot ring in solid sterling silver, *Charles* collection.

LEFT 'mth-02' ring in gold vermeil, *More Than This* collection.

RIGHT 'ch-02' long necklace in solid sterling silver, *Charles* collection.

BELOW Office/studio/home: Adeline Cacheux lives with her work.

ADELINE CACHEUX

Have you ever tried to find a jewelry collection that is so timeless and seemingly minimalist that it would work with every one of your outfits, regardless of the season or occasion? In other words, have you hankered after a collection of pure versatility that combines ease of wear with laid-back elegance? French designer Adeline Cacheux has been addressing this universal longing since 2007 by creating sleek chain bracelets, necklaces and earrings worked in solid sterling silver, gold and vermeil. 'It occurred to me that I never wore jewelry because I couldn't find the design I wanted!' she explains. 'I like accessories because they sit somewhere

between fashion and architecture. My background is in art history, and I used to work in contemporary galleries, so jewelry design gave me a chance to combine those two interests.' She adds, 'I consider jewelry to be a story that describes fluidity through a formal rather than intellectual approach.' Each of her pieces showcases an ingenious assembly of different chain types – fine geometric links can be teamed with larger links or clasps – and her work varies in bulkiness, leading to a highly effective use of proportion. She notes that 'the rock vibe that silver chains evoke doesn't necessarily rule out a sense of poetry and delicacy'. Christofle, the famous manufacturers of luxury silverware, soon recognized her potential and suggested a collaboration. Adeline's signature style, in balancing a low-key presence and underlying purity with cool edginess, transcends fashion trends and will be forever relevant. Her jewelry – the simplest ideas transformed into perfectly suave and wearable forms – introduces metal as a second skin.

www.adelinecacheux.com

ALYSSA NORTON

From cross-cultural pollination and ingenious dexterity emerges the ultimate in versatility: a necklace, bracelet, belt and headband in one. Alyssa Norton takes vintage materials, such as rhinestones and lace, and combines them with stones, chain beads and leather, all expertly braided, woven and twisted to forge covetable forms of body armour. The style unapologetically blends seeming contradictions – the classic with the bohemian and the high-end with the rough. It is precisely this unconventionality that makes Alyssa's work so appealing. She was introduced to jewelry making in 2000, when she attended the graduate programme at the Instituto Allende in Mexico. As a painter she studied the work of artists Dan Flavin and Donald Judd, inspiring her 'to explore how Perspex and geometric forms riveted to silver appeared to contain a light source from within'. She developed a passion for the anthropology of jewelry; 'how a piece holds multiple meanings for women, culture and society. Adornment says a lot about who a woman is, where she comes from, and her aspirations.' Alyssa notes that the energy of a piece drives her creative zeal. Inspired by archetypal elements of diverse cultural heritages – Japanese and Tibetan armour, say, or the African beading tradition – she creates modern accessories for women. 'The process is quite improvisational,' she explains. 'One of the first pieces I made that I would say completely expressed my aesthetic was a mixed materials piece, made of different shades of painted grey silk, sterling silver, rhinestones, painted grey leather and various oxidized chains. It tied around the wrist in a beautiful mess – it was hard to tell what was what. The bracelet had a complexity and aliveness to it. I felt what I was doing was relevant.' And that exact quality still prevails today in all Alyssa's works.

www.alyssanorton.com

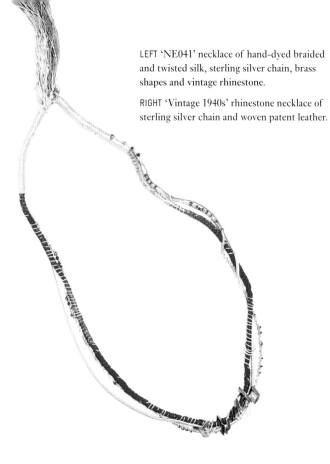

LEFT 'NE041' necklace of hand-dyed braided and twisted silk, sterling silver chain, brass shapes and vintage rhinestone.

RIGHT 'Vintage 1940s' rhinestone necklace of sterling silver chain and woven patent leather.

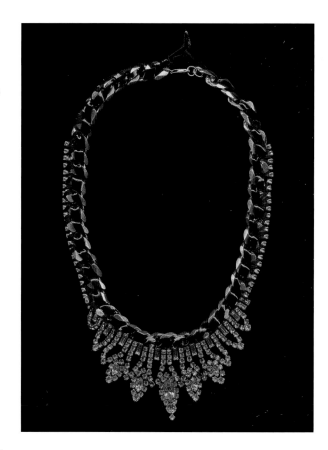

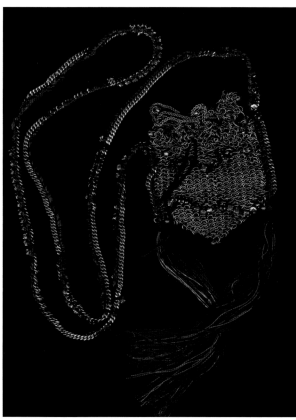

ABOVE Bangles in silk and cotton fabric wrapping with rhinestones.

LEFT 'Vintage Chain Maille' drawstring purse in braided silk, with rhinestone strap.

Necklace of gold beads, baby pearls and engraved South Sea pearl, *Knots* collection.

Bracelet of 7 cords, 18kt gold, diamonds and baby pearls, *Mix* collection.

Ring of 18kt yellow gold, South Sea pearl, diamond and rose-shaped coral, *Moving Stones* collection.

APRIATI

Step forward and be seduced by the power of Apriati's instant, easy-to-wear luxury. Trained in Italy, two young Greek designers Athina Axioti and Themis Bobolas have created a sought-after jewelry phenomenon that combines skilled artisanal craft, inspiration from Greek mythology and a tailor-made service. 'Everyone can wear an Apriati piece. We've developed a system in our pricing and design practice that enables people to acquire our creations according to their budget and taste,' they explain. This versatility places the label firmly in the sights of those who crave understated luxury. 'We wear our own creations, including a few pieces that we haven't taken off since we started designing. This is the Apriati spirit: designing jewelry that people live with and don't hide in a drawer,' they declare. 'We also provide a lifetime maintenance service, so people can enjoy our jewelry forever.' Their most emblematic design is probably the cord bracelet series, with small silver or diamond charms. Handcrafted in Athens in a selection of colours, each piece is unique, providing a modern and stylish amulet that can be worn as a single bracelet or stacked in multiples for maximum effect. The *7 Cords* collection, aptly named for the symbolism attributed to the number seven, exudes simplicity and elegance. The pair mix precious materials such as gold and diamonds with more casual materials to create a low-key, romantic brand that is also distinctly indulgent. Myths and wanderlust inspire the duo's creative journey. 'Our approach is a natural process of trial and error, discussion and hard work. The best way to describe what we do is *sur mesure*,' they explain. 'Nothing beats putting a smile on the face of a person wearing something specially designed for them.'

www.apriati.com

RIGHT Charms in the *Soul Cast* collection in rose and yellow gold worn on silk ties, and 'Stardust' bracelets in gold, sterling silver, diamonds and semi-precious stones.

BELOW A still life from the 2009 collection, with limited-edition pyrite necklaces with diamond beads and Mudra charm, and a bronze and black diamond 'Max' scarab belt buckle.

CATHERINE MICHIELS

To fully appreciate this fine, bohemian jewelry that evokes romantic heirlooms, you have to meet its free-spirited Belgian creator, the globetrotting Catherine Michiels. 'I was meant to live in eighteenth-century France,' she declares. 'My style never matches, but in all aspects of life – from my homes and studios to the items I wear – I'm a combination of the things I love: clothing and jewelry from many different cultures and periods.' A dream-catcher, her inspiration knows no boundaries of time, place or form. 'From the lavender colour of an old Paris Metro ticket to a stone-carved detail on a palazzo in Venice, every journey and encounter can become the catalyst for a new design,' she says.

To understand Catherine's drive you need to delve into the story of her extraordinary upbringing. One of her grandmothers often invited the writer Louise de Vilmorin for tea in her *petit château* just outside Brussels, greeting her wearing feathered mules and butterfly glasses adorned with crystals. The other grandmother owned a gallery on the north coast of Belgium. 'She sold costume jewelry,' recalls Catherine, 'which I helped her select when travelling salesmen visited.' Catherine's own tattoo-like charms and detailed pendants are like mystical amulets, each infused with Reiki, the spiritual healing technique that Catherine practices. 'From banker to biker, bourgeoise to rock star, yoga vegan to bon vivant, my customers are those who understand the message behind every piece so that it becomes their own style and story,' she states. 'I am honoured to have my friends become clients and my clients become friends.'

www.catherinemichiels.com

CLOCKWISE FROM RIGHT

'Anacapri' necklace in black agate, with 'Manon' cicada, 'Clara' eucalyptus pod, 'Ringo' yellow gold pendant with diamonds, pavé diamond mini oval charm and 'Fortuna' horn of abundance.

'The Sacred Cross' necklace of yellow gold and champagne diamonds.

'Juliette' photo-holder pendant of rose gold, champagne diamonds and sweetwater pearls.

'Lune Verte' one-of-a-kind ring of green moonstone and platinum.

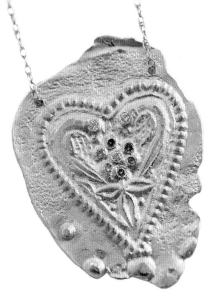

LEFT 'Antique Heart' necklace in 22kt gold, white and champagne diamonds, *Jaipur* collection.

BELOW Ensemble of pendant necklaces from the *Jaipur* and *Baroque* collections.

OPPOSITE ABOVE LEFT Reversible earrings (embellished each side) in 22kt gold, turquoise, rubies, white and blue diamonds, pearls and orange sapphire briolettes, *Negev* collection.

OPPOSITE ABOVE RIGHT Ensemble of 18kt and 22kt gold rings from the *Berbère*, *Negev*, *Constellation* and *Bijoux de Sentiments* collections.

OPPOSITE BELOW Chiselling a piece, held firm in concrete, with a custom-made mat tool to create a textural effect.

ESTHER

You could be deceived into thinking that the delicate yet battered and hammered golden trinkets that adorn Esther's jewelry are antique Etruscan archaeological treasures, museum relics of a past civilization, the raw beauty of the gold having been magically or sacredly endowed. But closer inspection reveals a subtle contemporary flair. These timeless, sensual creations are handmade and painstakingly chiselled by the goldsmith Esther Assouline. Mentored by master chiseller Wiga Mikulski, Esther has since become a sole practitioner who strives to resurrect the ancestral art of Middle Eastern chiselling. 'Technique should serve creativity, not the reverse,' she asserts. 'It shouldn't kill the soul of the piece.' Her Moroccan roots are at the core of her process. 'I designed my first ring, "Souvenir Berbère", in homage to my mother, and took inspiration from an antique engraved Berber bracelet that she was given by her own father.' Working directly onto raw 18kt and 22kt gold, Esther triumphs in rendering gem-encrusted surfaces that appeal precisely because of their roughness. 'I don't like all-in-one technical solutions,' she declares. 'My work has to be experimental and challenging, and definitely not polished.' Fragments of tourmalines, Tsavorite garnets and coloured diamonds act like rays of light, adding luxury to

the rough-hewn surfaces of her soulful designs. The intricate chiselled patterns will only reveal their full impact with age. 'Probably because of my colourist painting past, I now revel in the material, injecting it with a coloured life of its own,' states Esther. Hers is jewelry that enthrals the spirit through the eyes.

www.esther-fr.com

JACQUIE AICHE

The primordial earth-goddess Gaia must be rejoicing. Deftly handcrafted pieces in precious gold (the *Jacquie Aiche* fine jewelry line) and talismanic amulets (the *Blesslev* collection) pay homage to the hedonistic yet health-giving powers of minerals and gems. 'I love to use natural elements from the earth and transform them into wearable art,' says Jacquie. 'Above all, I enjoy hunting for rocks and crystals from all over the world. It's an organic experience. I choose the stone that speaks to me, or, as I like to think, the stone chooses me and the magic happens.' Jacquie's unerring ability to enhance the natural beauty of each gem or fossil

and to transform raw materials into fashionista covetables, speaks volumes about her deep connection to the medium and her talent for magnetizing the discerning crowds. Her background tells of diverse cultural influences – her father is Egyptian and her mother American Indian. A spiritual maverick herself, Jacquie describes a key encounter with Sylvain, 'a descendant of the revered mystics of North Africa', as a catalyst: 'He embraces a philosophy that started in the city of Breslev, Ukraine,' she explains. 'It heralds a message of joy and gratitude, and this is what triggered our collaboration.' This became the *Blesslev* collection. Describing herself as 'a gypsy at heart', Jacquie suggests that, 'if it were up to me, I would live in a huge tipi, barefoot, so I could always be a part of nature'. Not such a surprising admission, given that her jewelry is imbued with a natural hipness that softens the air of decadent sophistication and imparts a somewhat mischievous beauty. Jacquie inspires us to care about our world and to be thankful for life.

www.jacquieaiche.com

Necklace of 14kt rose gold, pavé diamond prong and raw pyrite, *Jacquie Aiche* collection.

Necklace of oval turquoise, polished stingray, 14kt pavé diamond teardrop and labradorite bezel on pyrite rondelles, *Blesslev* collection.

Necklace of 14kt yellow gold, pavé diamond and large teardrop turquoise, *Jacquie Aiche* collection.

CLOCKWISE FROM ABOVE

Earrings of 14kt yellow gold, pavé diamonds, and graduated raw green tourmaline, *Jacquie Aiche* collection.

'Chain Shower' earrings of 14kt rose gold, pavé partial diamonds and watermelon tourmaline slices, *Jacquie Aiche* collection.

Ring of 14kt rose gold, partial diamonds and trilobite fossil, *Jacquie Aiche* collection.

RIGHT Karen Liberman designing in
her Melbourne studio, which feels like
a stylish shop.

BELOW Ring of 18kt gold and emerald,
with rubies set in 22kt gold.

OPPOSITE ABOVE Necklace of aquamarines,
antique 18kt gold beads and ancient gold coin.

OPPOSITE BELOW Front and back of ring
of 14kt gold and grey diamond.

KAREN LIBERMAN

Karen Liberman's experience of travel and exotic cultures
has inspired her to emphasize traditional craft heritages in
her work, especially Indian jewelry-making traditions. Her
penchant for fine, detailed goldsmithing techniques points
to her Moroccan roots, while her Australian upbringing has
clearly influenced her chic bohemian signature style, devoid
of ostentation. 'It all begins with the stone, ancient bead
or old coin,' she says. 'Next I like to explore the different
options of adding layers to create a piece of jewelry that has
all the elements I would like it to express. These layers may
reference ancient jewelry-making practices or simply my
own personal sensory response to what combination of
materials works together beautifully.' Karen's love of a stone
is based on its distinctive, unique qualities, rather than on
what type of stone it is. For example, she favours opaque
diamonds, with all their flaws and great depth of character,
above traditional diamonds, which are sought after for their
clarity. She also promotes artisanal traditions by supporting
family-run businesses – the antithesis of mass manufacturing. 'I am very conscious that my work provides these
talented individuals with a livelihood,' she points out. Each
of her pieces is made timeless by nuances and a sense
of uniqueness that only dexterous handcraft can deliver.
Briolette-cut rubies, natural carved sapphires and ancient
coins – to name just a few precious materials – come together
as a classic yet soulful melody of rings, earrings and pendants in a style that echoes Karen's talent for a layered design
aesthetic. Her affinity with nature, beauty and local artistry
sings out through her work.

www.karenliberman.com.au

Pendant necklace of ancient bronze coin set in 24kt gold, fine handmade chain and sapphire beads.

Ring of hand-beaten 18kt gold and faceted blue sapphire.

Multi-wrap necklace of lapis lazuli, with 24kt gold clasp.

Ring of 18kt gold and carved emerald.

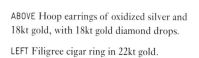

ABOVE Hoop earrings of oxidized silver and 18kt gold, with 18kt gold diamond drops.

LEFT Filigree cigar ring in 22kt gold.

OPPOSITE, CLOCKWISE FROM TOP LEFT

'Long Necklace I' of 10 microns of 24kt yellow gold vermeil and white diamonds, with 18kt gold chain.

'Ring VII' of 18kt yellow gold and white diamonds.

'Ring IX' of 10 microns of 24kt yellow gold vermeil and white diamonds.

'Ring I' of 18kt yellow gold and black diamonds.

'Double Ring X' of 10 microns of 24kt yellow gold vermeil and white diamonds, with 18kt yellow gold chain.

RIGHT Lara Melchior's workspace, with its creative anthropologist/biologist feel.

BELOW 'Double Ring IV' of 18kt yellow gold and white diamonds.

LARA MELCHIOR

The pleasure of wearing a gossamer-thin piece of gold jewelry is heightened by the mesmerizing visual delicacy of ornate filigree metalwork. Small brown or white diamonds and rubies gently punctuate irregular honeycombed surfaces, as if a mysterious messenger has left a trail of precious stones in his wake, while rings and pendants sport an overlay of golden petals in an organic cluster on lace-like metal. It should be noted that designer Lara Melchior, inspired by Gustav Klimt's 'Golden Phase' and by the Fauvist movement, almost missed her vocation: 'I used to be an illustrator and fashion photographer,' she confides. 'Then one day I

started making fancy jewelry for friends. I liked it until I grew bored and unfocused. Fortunately I decided to learn goldsmithing, sensing the promise that working gold would open infinite possibilities, and I've never looked back.' Surrounded by unusual artifacts, including a spectacular taxidermy peacock, Lara has created a small workshop where she can peacefully solder, polish and file her graceful yet ultra-cool work. 'My first collection is stocked by Colette, the famous shop in Paris, and it's been a blessing. I worked on it for over a year, and I have learned from my mistakes. Today I try to ground my creative style by including timeless signature pieces that can reappear in each new collection.' The modernity of Lara's approach goes hand in hand with a slight hint of archaeology, of Afghan tribal jewelry craft. A chic Parisian herself, Lara designs with versatility and effortless wearability in mind because, as she whispers, 'A good piece of jewelry should let the wearer not worry about it, while it works its magic.'

www.laramelchior.com

BELOW 'Light My Fire' cuff of sterling silver, black rhodium and white diamonds.

RIGHT 'Lilith' earrings of 18kt black gold and white diamonds.

BOTTOM Sanding the cast gold to give it a smooth aspect.

OPPOSITE, FROM TOP

'Precious' medallion necklace of sterling silver, black rhodium and white diamonds.

'Tess' ring of 18kt white gold and white diamonds.

'Once Upon a Time' necklace of 18kt white gold and white diamonds.

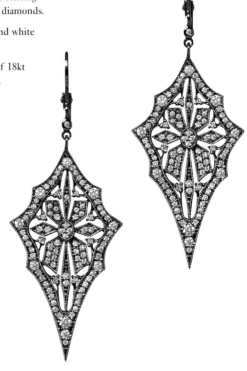

STONE

Bring some filigree glamour to your daily life with these easy-to-wear and finely crafted heirlooms of the future. By combining old techniques, which only a few jewelry work-shops in Paris can accomplish, with the monochromatic modernity of diamonds set on white, black and rose gold or silver rhodium, Stone propels fine jewelry into a cool and subtly edgy style arena. The company was originally launched in 2004 by Marie Poniatowski and Vanessa de Jaegher. The self-taught Marie, who now runs the company, had long been exposed to high-end fashion and luxury, and this prompted her to develop a strong aesthetic vision and creative strategy from the start. She notes, 'My father's responsibilities, when I was a child, as head of French *Vogue*, surely helped to sharpen my fascination for anything beautiful.' She was in New York when she was struck by the realization that, by comparison, the fine-jewelry scene in Paris was defined by 'Place Vendôme' elitism. The time had come to introduce to Paris 'a brand of accessible jewels for women; precious pieces that behave like a second skin'. Moroccan-inspired patterns make each piece luxurious yet appropriate for everyday wear. The hotly sought-after *micro pavage* technique is combined with a contemporary rock vibe, which borrows judiciously from biker and goth narratives. Think of what your inner teenage girl would long for: Edwardian exquisiteness sprinkled with a touch of rebellious iconography. A willingness to experiment is also what keeps Stone at the forefront. Marie recalls that the 'Precious' medallion – first worked in silver rhodium with big rose-cut diamonds – was 'the most imposing piece I ever made'. She says she designs for herself first and foremost, 'then I hope that the elegant and modern women of this world will follow suit'. No doubt they'll happily queue for a piece of this casual chic with a twist.

http://stoneparis.com

'Ampule' necklace of sterling silver and 18kt gold.

'Double Cross' earrings of oxidized sterling silver and 18kt gold.

'File' rings of 18kt rose gold and 14kt green gold.

'Gold Blanket Cross' earrings of 18kt vermeil and enamel.

'Star' earrings in 18kt gold.

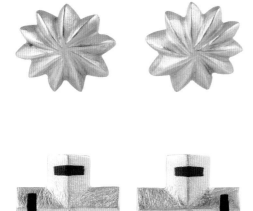

BOTTOM A wall of patterns and prints that remind designer Kate Jones of all the places she has lived, and their influences which she carries with her.

BELOW Collect, stack, cherish: Ursa Major's jewelry will accompany you anytime, anywhere.

URSA MAJOR

'Less is more' describes so many aspects of Ursa Major, the subtle jewelry collection designed by Kate Jones. Let's start with the exploration of simple lines that make up far from basic geometric compositions. Then there is an infusion of understated allure that makes ring- or bracelet-stacking all the more befitting. Here is a contemporary vibe that exudes agelessness thanks to a tribal varnish. 'I am largely inspired by lines: the curve of a window moulding, the rise and fall of a mountain crest, the arm of a favourite chair,' Kate shares. Of her working process she says, 'I like to solve the idea of a piece pretty thoroughly before I start on the prototype.

But, once I'm carving the wax, I always leave room for organic change, watching the piece as I'm building it and making changes in response.' Metalsmithing is at the core of Kate's pursuit: enamel gives a touch of colour, and recycled gold provides a precious canvas for her keepsakes. 'Despite switching to study textiles and fashion along the way, I've always returned to metalsmithing. It's the medium that suits me the most, as I'm extremely detail-oriented and most comfortable working on a small scale,' she confides. 'I'm currently working on a collection based on eroded, deteriorated sculpture and architecture. Think marble statues with broken limbs, half-faced sandstone lions, and elaborate cornices smoothed out by the elements.' Informing her art with references to history, Kate fashions a quiet but meaningful luxury, the rare kind that cuts through fashion cycles and shines through time like a constellation, honouring its stellar namesake.

www.ursamajorcollection.com

SCULPTURAL BLISS

Architectural prowess enhances creative ingenuity.
Precious jewelry of the sharpest kind.

ALEXANDRA JEFFORD

What began as a fascination with the shapes and colours associated with geology has grown into an ambitious offering of collectable jewelry designs. Each one-off piece, designed and handmade by Alexandra Jefford, is a contemporary masterpiece of elegant poise, graphic structuralism and expressive style. Often described as sculptural or geological curiosities, her work exudes femininity via organic references and a selection of spellbinding gems – pear-shaped grey diamonds, Paraiba tourmalines, black opals, emeralds and grey pearls. Alexandra was born and raised in Geneva, then moved to England to study fine art at Central St Martins, and has now been designing jewelry in her London studio for over a decade. 'Jewelry has to live on and off the body, like living sculpture,' she notes. She essentially designs for herself, test-running each creation before releasing it to the public. An idea usually comes from something that she is yearning for and would like to possess. 'I then get attached to a piece emotionally, and certain ones are hard to part with – hence I'm a really bad salesperson,' she laughs. Alexandra's creative approach is based on a multi-dimensional pursuit of innovative forms, textures and conceptual ideas. 'I also have slight obsessions about certain subjects I definitely want to incorporate in my pieces. I don't

really like revisiting old styles, but I'm always in search of the new, perfect jewel,' she explains. And there is absolutely no doubt that she will find it.

www.alexandrajefford.com

RIGHT 'Specks and Fragments' ring of 18kt white gold, large black Tahitian baroque pearl and carved piece of Maw-sit-sit jadeite, *Movement* collection.

BELOW 'Walter' ring of 18kt white gold, carved green opal and emerald, *Movement* collection.

ABOVE 'Le Rendez-Vous' bracelet of 18kt white gold and pavé diamonds.

RIGHT 'Berry in the Bush' ring of 18kt white gold, 18kt yellow gold leaf, golden South Sea pearl and diamonds.

CLOCKWISE FROM TOP LEFT *Little People Pendants* series: 'Diaghilev' in quartz, lapis lazuli, coral and 18kt yellow gold; 'Nijinska' in angel's skin coral, sunstone, quartz, kynite and 18kt yellow gold; 'Bakst' in baroque pearls, Burmese jade, moss and white agates, and 18kt yellow gold; 'Tourmanova' in cultured Tahitian pearl, Mediterranean coral, rainbow obsidian, brilliant-cut diamond, rose wood and 18kt yellow gold; 'Pepita' in ebony, lignum vitae, malachite, baroque pearl and 18kt yellow gold; 'Nijinski' in rock crystal, Mediterranean coral, moonstone, grey agate, brilliant-cut diamond and 18kt yellow gold; 'Balanchine' in agate, jasper, lapis lazuli and 18kt yellow gold; 'Folkine' in quartz, jasper, amber and 18kt yellow gold.

RIGHT 'Cupido' one-off earrings of matching trapiche emeralds, antique banded agate, amber and 18kt yellow gold.

FAR RIGHT 'Poiret' pins of 18kt yellow gold, with marble grey agate, bright chrysoprase, pink phosphorsiderite and faceted grey moonstone.

BELOW RIGHT The *pièce de résistance*: a custom-made display cabinet in Belmacz's showroom and studio in London.

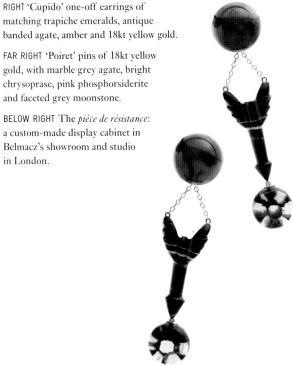

BELMACZ

Heralding a maker of flamboyant jewelry, whose inventions comprise a contemporary cabinet of precious curiosities. Past and present co-exist through near-anthropological experimentation and modernist shapes. Julia Muggenburg, creator of Belmacz, is a pioneer who delights in sensual beauty and global tribalism. 'I love the special allure of jewels – the lively colours of gemstones, the patina of silver, the gleam of gold,' she confides. 'Design is my mission. I aspire to art and its aspects. One must never forget that jewels are objects that are used and need to be shown off. The process of creating a jewel involves the combination of imagination and craft – a special accommodation between artistry and industry.' Turning dormant raw materials into polished signature pieces, each different and alive, is what captivates Julia. German-born, she studied fine art at Central St Martins, and launched Belmacz in her adopted city, London – a place which, more than any other, nurtures and applauds avant-gardists. Her own quixotic fashion style is, she laughs, 'a bit of Matisse and Marlene Dietrich, and a bit of Armageddon, mixed together with rouge and the indispensable scent of Belmacz No. 1'. This formula gives a good indication of the exhilarating creativity at play in her work. Belmacz jewels are crafted in limited series of eight

and most are one-of-a-kind wonders that elevate sculptural chic and luxurious novelty to new heights. 'I want to create pieces that are as individual as they are indulgent, as eccentric as they are wearable; objects that articulate an emotion, yet intrigue with their powerful mystery,' she explains. Julia is a master of saying the most with the least.

www.belmacz.com

ABOVE 'Sautoire' necklace of 18kt yellow gold, yellow cultured South Sea pearls, sapphires and antique Mediterranean coral.

RIGHT 'A. B. Toklas' ring of 18kt yellow gold and Mediterranean coral.

RIGHT 'Augustus' one-off brooch of 18kt yellow gold, hawk's eye, amber, pink opal, chrysoprase and Tahitian blue cultured pearl.

BELOW 'Mandarin' ring of 18kt gold, rose rutilated quartz and rose quartz.

BOTTOM 'Mombassa' ring of chrysoprase, rock crystal and gold leaf.

DEBORAH PAGANI

What is the link between Cleopatra, the Chrysler building and Grace Jones? Answer: confident, statement jewelry that kicks instant wow-factor allure to stratospheric levels on the style scale. New York-based designer Deborah Pagani works an unconventional mix of pyramidal architecture, polished surfaces and radiant gems, inscribing into each of her creations' DNA hints of Art Deco and echoes of great entertainment icons (Joan Crawford, Bette Davis, Rita Hayworth). We are most definitely in glamazon territory here, with names that refer, almost fetishistically, to powerful female figures ('Queen Bee', 'Zeena' and 'Patra'), and with a few dark rock 'n' roll innuendos thrown in for good measure (as in 'Gotham'). 'If Cleopatra were living in New York City in the modern day,' Deborah speculates, 'she would wear my jewelry. It embodies all of the qualities she possessed, particularly sophistication and power.' Paradoxically, the strong referential backdrop to her collections does not intimidate; rather, it comforts. The underlying feminine quality guarantees effortless wearability and elegance. This is jewelry that elevates rather than overpowers a woman's personality. 'I knew the extremes of jewelry – the trendy, momentary designs that fade out, and the classic ornamental style – so my desire was to find a balance between the two. I wanted to design fine jewelry that a woman could incorporate into her style without it seeming contrived,' Deborah explains. 'I envisaged my creative style as bringing the 1930s and Rock together, and Art Deco was the common denominator. It was valid that my designs should incorporate elements of it, while making it my own.' And make it her own she most certainly has, inventing her own futuristic rendition, and licensing a woman's ultra-sensuality at the same time. Quite a feat.

www.deborahpagani.com

CLOCKWISE FROM TOP

'Anita' pendant of 18kt white gold, dandrite 'Snowflake' agate and grey diamonds, *Queen Bee* collection.

'Idol' earrings of 18kt oxidized gold, black diamonds and lapis lazuli, *Patra* collection.

'Pyramid' cuff of 18kt oxidized gold and white diamonds, *Queen Bee* collection.

'Gotham' ring of 18kt white gold, grey diamonds and grey moonstone, *Patra* collection.

ELENA VOTSI

Eros, Greek god of love and desire, surely presided over the creation of Elena Votsi's award-winning 'Precious Love' ring: a geometrical wonder, whose diamond-paved plateau is pierced by a fine arrow, a single garnet drop depicting the moment of bloody impact. Elena has a deep appreciation of her own cultural heritage, which in turn provides her with abundant source material. Inspired by the permanent collections of such eminent institutions as the Acropolis Museum, Benaki Museum, Cycladic Art Museum and National Gallery, her jewelry is now sold in the gift shops of each of these venues. Reminiscing about her childhood

on the island of Hydra, and subsequent summer visits back home, she recalls: 'Its harbour looked like a theatre. I admired the women in their best clothes and jewelry, parading like elegant protagonists of a fictional play. I knew I wanted to become a jewelry artist.' The proportions of her pieces are voluminous yet perfectly balanced; lines are clean but architecturally sophisticated; surfaces are polished though emotionally charged. 'There are times when I develop jewelry around themes such as a ball, a heart, light or shadow. At other times I'm drawn by a material – yellow gold, iron, diamonds or white marble – or by a random shape, or colour, or a beautiful morning light,' Elena explains. 'But what drives me above all is the fact that I can transform a cold, hard, raw material into a piece of jewelry, which will eventually come to life when worn by a woman.' In addition to winning prestigious awards (including Couture 2009 and 2011 in Las Vegas), Elena's greatest achievements include designing the medals for the Olympic Games in Athens in 2004 (the front of the medal will be used in all future Olympic Games). The gods of Mount Olympus have found a perfect earthly ambassador in the person of Elena Votsi.

www.elenavotsi.com

RIGHT 'Sparkle Shapes' earrings of 18kt yellow gold, and black and white brilliant-cut diamonds, *Bales* collection.

BELOW 'Sparkle Shapes' ring of 18kt yellow gold, South Sea pearl and brilliant-cut diamonds, *Bales* collection.

RIGHT 'Precious Love' ring of 18kt yellow gold, white brilliant-cut diamonds and garnet, *Unique Pieces* collection.

ABOVE RIGHT 'Purple Cross' pendant of 18kt yellow gold and amethyst, *Shape* collection.

LEFT 'Double Pearl Shackle' bracelet of 18kt yellow gold and black Akoya pearls, *It's Only Rock 'n' Roll* collection.

BELOW 'Vincent's Empty Sovereign' ring of 18kt yellow gold and hand-cut blue/black sapphires, *Vincent* collection.

BOTTOM Filing away all imperfections after a piece has come back from casting, and before it is polished.

HANNAH MARTIN

'Fashioning luxury jewelry for men that girlfriends will steal' is Hannah Martin's singular creative pursuit. Whether the men will allow it is another story, and the only menacing note in a highly successful enterprise. 'The focus is entirely on sculpture for the body. The details are consistently masculine, but the sculpture is always the defining part of my work,' says Hannah. 'I was studying at Central St Martins, on the foundation year of sculpture, when I decided to leave: I somehow knew it wasn't my calling. But I returned to study for a BA Honours in jewelry design ... at which point I knew in my heart that I'd found my passion.'

Hannah's powerful talent is all about forging sculptural and unconventional designs that are future collectables, finding the perfect match of stone and metal that will bring her designs to life, and formulating glorious colour brews. Her work is outstanding for its technical skill and refinement: only the finest craftsmen in London are used, and each piece goes through an average of seven processes, from initial moulding to setting and polishing. In this respect, *The Man Who Knows Everything* collection has probably been Hannah's biggest challenge so far. 'The rings are entirely triangular – a pyramid, in fact – with my signature facet and sharp edges,' she explains. Balancing a futuristic edginess (underlined by the option to 'try on' the jewelry on her website via ingenious augmented-reality technology) with baroque titles (as in 'Euphoria of Lights' or 'The Forgotten Treasure of the Infamous Aguila Dorada'), Hannah pushes the potential of jewelry beyond the limits of traditional aesthetics, and thereby redefines the concept of luxury. It may be enough to combine the 'Alpha Fe-' with 'Male'.

www.hannahmartinlondon.com

'Heavy Shackle' bangle of 18kt yellow gold and orange sapphires, *The Forgotten Treasure of the Infamous Aguila Dorada* collection.

'Shaman's Triangle' pavé cufflinks of 18kt yellow gold, orange sapphires and rubies, *The Man Who Knows Everything* collection.

'Euphoria of Lights: The Comte's Pyramid' ring of 18kt red gold, rubies, orange sapphires and tourmalines, *The Man Who Knows Everything* collection.

'Twisted Shackle' ring of 18kt red and yellow gold, and brown diamonds, *The Forgotten Treasure of the Infamous Aguila Dorada* collection.

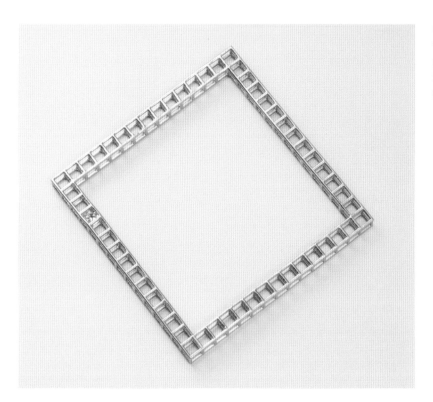

JACQUELINE RABUN

A piece of jewelry can have many qualities – sentimental, ornamental, celebratory, for example – but only rarely does it convey a special mood: inner peace. Contemplating a Jacqueline Rabun creation, let alone wearing one, inspires a near-religious experience. Take her *Cave* collection: this early work, designed for Georg Jensen in 2001, 'engages the wearer to seek tranquillity and retreat to an inner space for stillness and contemplation'. The interplay between organic and geometric lines, immaculate surfaces and ingenious construction renders the sculptural concepts behind each miniature artwork. A prime example is the *Beautiful*

collection, which 'symbolizes the importance of unity in a relationship while maintaining a sense of individuality'. The ring and bangle consist of three movable parts: two spherical outer pieces and a slender centrepiece. Jacqueline knew she would be a jeweler when she discovered the work of contemporary American designers, including Ted Muehling, Robert Lee Morris and Gabriella Kiss. 'My style is a fusion of architectural, poetic and organic influences. I've been designing for over twenty years. My first works were very organic and very raw, using mostly silver. My design language is now more refined and emotive, predominantly in 18kt yellow gold,' Jacqueline explains. Born in Germany to American parents, she was raised in California. In 1990 she established her brand, soon after moving to London, which was where she began her long-term collaboration with Georg Jensen. In 2007 she opened her showroom in a converted stables in Belgravia. Only a true design choreographer could have brought to life such exquisite, meaningful compositions – no fuss or frills but brimming with subtlety and intelligence. The talent of a smooth operator.

www.jacquelinerabun.com

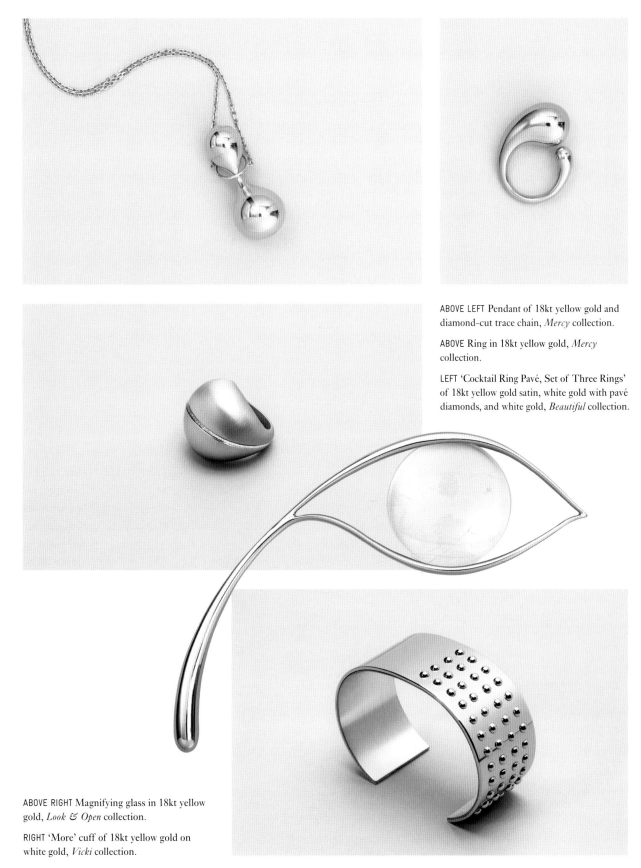

ABOVE LEFT Pendant of 18kt yellow gold and diamond-cut trace chain, *Mercy* collection.

ABOVE Ring in 18kt yellow gold, *Mercy* collection.

LEFT 'Cocktail Ring Pavé, Set of Three Rings' of 18kt yellow gold satin, white gold with pavé diamonds, and white gold, *Beautiful* collection.

ABOVE RIGHT Magnifying glass in 18kt yellow gold, *Look & Open* collection.

RIGHT 'More' cuff of 18kt yellow gold on white gold, *Vicki* collection.

LEFT AND BOTTOM RIGHT 'Peanut' necklace (closed and open) of 18kt yellow gold and South Sea golden pearl: Mrzyk & Moriceau design, signed and numbered.

BOTTOM LEFT 'Patacorp' pendant of 18kt yellow gold and white diamonds: Geneviève Gauckler design, signed and numbered.

BELOW 'Cœur' pendant of 18kt yellow and white gold, diamonds and rubies: Geneviève Gauckler design.

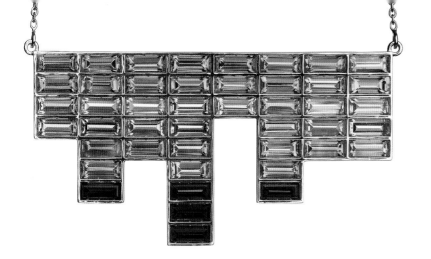

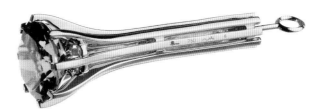

LE BUISSON

A shrub, *un buisson* in French, is a humble yet fuller version of a tree – a discreet but necessary feature of any landscape, providing a rich ecosystem that nurtures hidden species. With a similar desire for discretion and aversion to ostentation, Le Buisson reflects back on jewelry as intimate talisman, with both simplicity and playfulness. Founded by Michèle Monory and Francis Fichot, the project is a unique grouping of talents (initially renowned in interior and industrial design but with no previous knowledge of jewelry making). Together, they shed a brand-new light on an established industry. According to contributor Matali Crasset, the company gives 'novice designers a free hand to create from scratch, thus inadvertently pushing the boundaries of jewelry making in tandem with skilled artisans'. She adds, 'We offer unique, precious pieces that are very easy to wear at any time of day.' With unorthodox perspectives and exuberant viewpoints, the designers explore the sparkle and luminescence of gems through the study of movement and light (the *Mobilité* series, and *Equaliseur* and *Torche* series by Matali Crasset); the relationship between visibility and concealment (in Mrzyk & Moriceau's *Peanut* and *Sextime* series, familiar forms harbour surprises, such as traditionally showcased precious elements being hidden from view);

and the representation of symbolic signature figures worked in gold (Geneviève Gauckler's elementally shaped but far from innocent characters, such as Thermokukus and Patacorp). These are creations that revolutionize jewelry by refusing to appeal to vanity but instead restoring the sincere and often secretive affection that bonds a wearer with his or her prized bauble.

www.lebuissonparis.fr

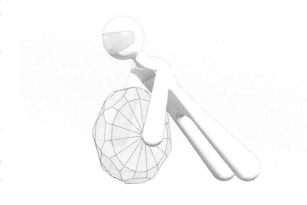

OPPOSITE ABOVE 'Triangle' necklace of 12mm freshwater pearls and oxidized silver chains.

OPPOSITE BELOW LEFT 'Double Shell' ring of ascending peacock pearls and 18kt white gold.

OPPOSITE BELOW RIGHT 'Pinkie Shell' ring of peacock pearl and 18kt white gold.

RIGHT 'Sliced' earrings of 10mm peacock pearls and 18kt yellow gold.

BELOW Most of Melanie Georgacopoulos's pearls undergo processes of mechanical engineering: here, a selection of 12mm white pearls is being drilled.

MELANIE GEORGACOPOULOS

According to *The Book of The Pearl* (1908) by renowned mineralogist George Frederick Kunz, pearls are 'perfected by Nature and requiring no art to enhance their beauty'. But there's an exception to the rule. The work of Greek designer Melanie Georgacopoulos revisits pearls via a unique creative approach. Her pearls are sliced, distressed and combined with contrasting coloured halves. A multitude of innovative techniques and methods of display are used to create modern and highly sculptural ensembles that nevertheless retain the pearl's long-cherished appeal as a symbol of purity and longevity. 'I always start designing on paper, drawing mainly geometric shapes,' says Melanie. 'Once I'm happy with a design, I start working on prototypes, which is one of my favourite stages – choosing the materials and scale, adjusting on the body so that, no matter how big or complex the piece, it always feels comfortable.' Melanie studied sculpture for four years before embracing jewelry. 'I love the fact that jewelry is a wearable object that is so close to the body; and I love how significant it can be,' she muses. Her magic lies in her ability to create elegant yet deceptively classic works of art: a regal ring made of a striking juxtaposition of pearls of different sizes; a bracelet consisting of a single strand of white pearls that becomes double as the pearls are sliced open, exposing their bare core; a necklace composed of black strings, like a delicate harp, each end terminating in a white pearl; and a modern rendition of an opulent, antique collar, recalling the nobility of the resting wings of a black swan. The subdued iridescence of pearls, their lustre and format, are beautified through Melanie's visionary talent. Once described as 'the tears of angels', pearls have now been metamorphosed into tears of joy.

www.melaniegeorgacopoulos.com

OPPOSITE, FROM TOP

'Arlequin' necklace of recomposed 12mm white and peacock pearls.

'Sliced' collar necklace of 10mm peacock freshwater pearls, with white pearl and 18kt yellow gold clasp.

'Onyx Encrusted' necklace of 12mm white freshwater pearls with faceted onyx and 18kt yellow gold clasp.

'Sliced' bracelet of 10mm white freshwater pearls, with gold-plated magnetic clasp.

ABOVE 'Palm Tree' necklace of 3mm peacock and white pearls.

BELOW 'Cube Chain Neckpiece with Floating Tahitian Pearls' of 18kt gold and Tahitian pearls, *Cube* collection.

BOTTOM LEFT 'Tower' one-off ring of 18kt gold, raw cognac diamond octahedron, diamond baguettes and floating cultured pearl.

BOTTOM RIGHT 'Zig Zag' earrings of 18kt gold, aquamarine and chrysoberyl, *Spinning Stone* collection.

LEFT 'Ferris Wheel' earrings of 18kt palladium white gold, black diamond briolettes and white sapphire, *Ferris Wheel* collection.

BELOW RIGHT 'Double Spinning Stone' bracelet of 14kt palladium white gold and pink amethysts, *Spinning Stone* collection.

BOTTOM Not a traditional jeweler's bench, but a fabulous heavy old worktable: Patricia Madeja adds luminescent beads to a framework, inspired by hanging lamps seen in a design magazine.

PATRICIA MADEJA

Combining strong geometric forms with skilfully engineered movement, Patricia Madeja's jewelry suggests a world of skyscrapers, bridges, roller coasters and ferris wheels. Her bold architectural references are offset by coloured stones that temper the angular edges and animate each structure to give a dazzling, lighthouse effect. 'My original intention was to study architecture, but after being accepted to both Pratt Institute's School of Architecture and School of Art & Design, I chose to pursue an education in the visual arts, focusing on 2D design, which didn't serve me well. My strength was in 3D design,' Patricia confides. 'I transferred

to sculpture and then struggled miserably with scale. After taking a jewelry class, I just knew this was my medium. I could create comfortably, my detail-oriented nature was perfectly challenged, and I could make functional, object-based work that appealed to my practical nature.' Always with sketchbook in hand, Patricia translates her inspirations onto paper. She then constructs models directly in metal, mainly using square wire, sizing stock and sheet metal. She also makes models in order to create exact replicas of particular components. 'Hand-building each link would result in too much variation. Most often I combine the two processes to execute a piece and overcome its challenges, such as constructing a clasp that is completely integrated into the design. The clasp creation can sometimes take longer than making the piece itself,' she notes. All her designs build on previous variations, which ensures cohesiveness and renewal. Visiting her West Islip studio in New York, one is struck by the unexpectedly non-hi-tech, 'antique'-looking environment – a far cry from her work, which is mathematical, precise and highly polished. The amusing contradiction makes her technical precision and attention to detail all the more scintillating.

www.patriciamadeja.com

BELOW 'Algorithmic Quartz' bracelet of resin dipped in 22kt gold.

RIGHT A scientific approach: sketch research for the *Algorithmic Quartz* collection.

BOTTOM 'Algorithmic Quartz' set of two rings in 18kt gold and carbon deposition on silver.

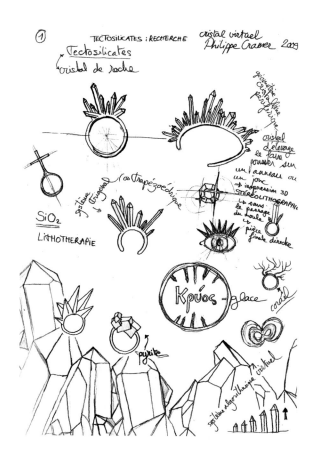

PHILIPPE CRAMER

A creative multi-tasker, an insatiable experimenter and learner, a stylist, a designer and an artist, all in equal measure … Philippe Cramer applies the same rigorous vision to all his design projects, whether jewelry, furniture, home accessories or interiors. He treats his works as small sculptures and ensures that everything is impeccably made. 'I avoid extensive surface decoration and intricate detailing, which take away from the visual impact,' he notes. He is, however, open-minded in his creative process. 'Some pieces will start from wax that I have hand-carved. Others will stem from an intellectual concept, challenging my jeweler and myself to explore unusual techniques or proportions.' Philippe works indiscriminately with wood, metal, ceramics and plastics, using handcraft methods or industrial techniques, or a combination of both. His approach is often scientific: 'For the past few years, I've been experimenting with physical vapour deposition to coat gold with radiant colours.' He has also worked with Play-Doh, sculpting organic shapes and then dipping them in gold. 'My latest endeavour is working with hand-blown glass sprinkled with diamonds. The next one will be investigating microstructures found on butterfly wings and beetle shells in order to understand colour refraction.' Geneva-based, with dual Swiss and American nationality, Philippe founded his company, Cramer and Cramer, in 2001. Two years later he opened a showroom in the heart of Geneva's contemporary art world. The 'Made in Switzerland' label, carried by all his products, is an important part of their identity. But while the materials and craftsmanship have to be excellent, the end product does not need to look expensive. It all comes down to a pared-down luxury, which Philippe summarizes as 'a sensual minimalism for contemporary and elegant living'.

www.philippecramer.com / www.philippecramershop.com

CLOCKWISE FROM RIGHT

'Aare' rings in 18kt gold, with amethyst, garnet and citrine.

'Rhone' bracelets of 18kt gold, garnet and green sapphires, and 18kt gold and citrine.

'Gold Dipped' bracelet of handcarved wood, sandblasted and dipped in 22kt gold.

'Gold Dipped' ring of hardened Play-Doh, dipped in 22kt gold.

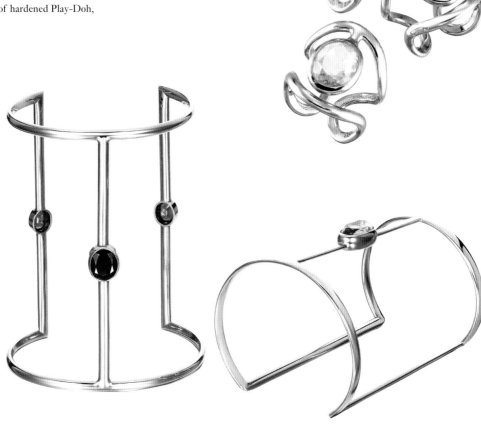

BELOW Four discs of red gold and black acrylic glass, *Loop's Rings* collection.

BOTTOM 'Ring #4' in black rhodium-plated 925 sterling silver, *Wendepunkt* collection.

TOP 'Jewelry for Ear 1' in gold-plated 925 sterling silver, *Wendepunkt* collection.

ABOVE 'Bangle #5' in white acrylic glass, *Wendepunkt* collection.

SIBYLLE KRAUSE

A perfect synthesis of form and meaning. There are few motifs in jewelry sculpture that can rival the simplicity and effectiveness of the infinity symbol: a visual shorthand infused with spiritual and philosophical meaning. In *Wendepunkt* ['Turning Point'], German designer Sibylle Krause guides a single lithe band of precious metal to twist gently in curvaceous whirls that have no end or beginning – a perfect full circle in cast and galvanized silver. Sibylle explains that she is always on the lookout for things that are pleasingly shaped, 'especially things that appear simple at first sight, yet are deeply complex. My work is to give a

piece of jewelry the ultimate shape, so that its function is fulfilled and it matches a person's character perfectly.' She adds, 'My mission is to underline the wearer's individuality, not to confer a new personality on her or him.' Sibylle trained as a goldsmith at the Staatliche Zeichenakademie Hanau, then moved to Vicenza in Italy to work with The Fifth Season jewelry company. She went on to study design at Pforzheim University, which enabled her to develop her knowledge of jewelry and everyday objects. A further stint at the Kookmin University of Seoul introduced her to the clarity, harmony and deceptive simplicity of Asian design and culture – characteristics that she has clearly carried over into her own work. 'Inspired by mathematical curves, the Möbius strip, the aspect of positive and negative versus light and shadow, my creative style is a language,' she says. 'As a young designer, my goal is that my touch can be immediately identifiable, yet always surprisingly fresh.' All the boxes have already been ticked.

www.sibylle-krause.de

YUNUS & ELIZA

Masked actors, illustrious heroes and tragic figures with poetic silhouettes lend a phantasmal presence to the unfolding of what appears to be a dramatic opera or epic Venetian ball. These are 'sculptures to be worn', according to their genius creators, artist Yunus Ascott and sculptor Eliza Higginbottom. Although not formally trained in jewelry making, the pair have joined demiurgic forces to tailor their creative skills to a miniature scale, without losing any of the intensity and sensuality of their subject matter. 'We merge the boundaries between fashion, art and jewelry. Our signature sculptural collections juxtapose mythology with a

futuristic twist,' they explain. 'We create a luxurious world immersed in lyrical combinations. Classical fine features, subtle and luminous, are contrasted with raw and dark realities, while fragmented remains metamorphose into graceful hybrid beings.' Recent experimentation with colour via transparent and luminous enamel has contributed extra decadence and a quality finish to the work, while also accentuating the presence of precious metal. 'Working with gold – fair-trade – is very rewarding: it's so pliant and giving. When we're making our large couture headpieces we do a lot of welding of various metals, and the immediacy of being able to work like this is very satisfying. Watching silver solder flow is, without fail, enthralling,' they share. Clients and the fashion and jewelry industries alike have been quick to heap praise: Yunus & Eliza won the British Fashion Council/*ELLE* magazine Talent Launch Pad in 2010 and the Treasure Designer of the Year at London Jewelry Week 2011. A well-deserved standing ovation for the dramatists behind these ceremonial, fantastical productions.

www.yunus-eliza.co.uk

CLOCKWISE FROM LEFT

Front and back views of the 'Y&E Goddess' ring of 24kt gold-plated sterling silver with translucent red enamel, *Beyond the Darkness* collection.

'Child Prodigy' ring of 24kt gold-plated sterling silver and Swarovski crystals, *Beyond the Darkness* collection.

'Child Prodigy' pendant of 18kt gold-plated sterling silver with jet-black enamel, *Beyond the Darkness* collection.

LEFT 'Black Swan' necklace of 18kt gold-plated sterling silver, black enamel claws, glossy black feather wings, with long gold-filled chain, *There Was Flight* collection.

BELOW LEFT 'Poseidon' ring in sterling silver, *Unsung Heroes* collection.

BELOW RIGHT 'Goddess Tears' pendant in 18kt gold-plated sterling silver, *There Was Flight* collection.

OPPOSITE ABOVE Three views of the 'Dali Puppet' ring of 24kt gold-plated sterling silver with jet-black enamel, *Beyond the Darkness* collection.

OPPOSITE BELOW 'Claw Drop' pendant of 18kt gold-plated sterling silver, black enamel feather work and long gold-filled chain, and 'Hawk Armor' necklace of 18kt gold-plated sterling silver and long gold-filled chain, *There Was Flight* collection.

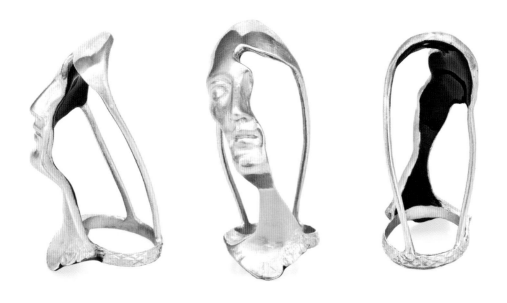

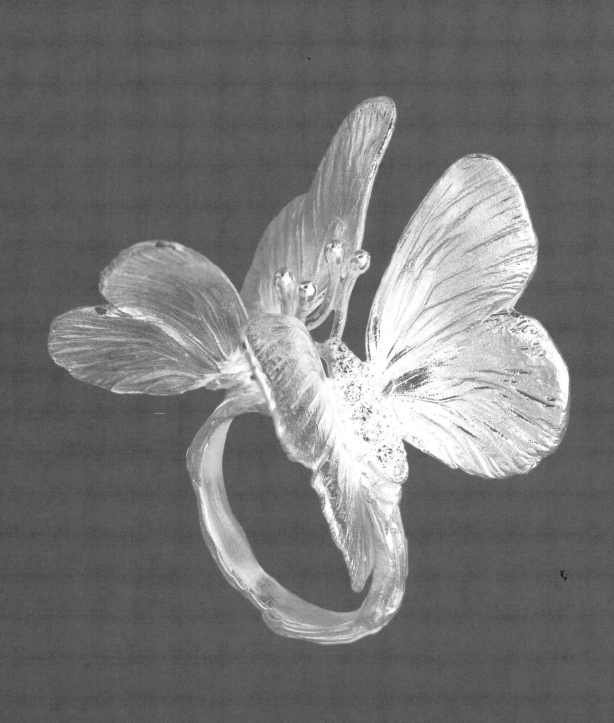

THE
DELECTABLES

Precious and playful delights straight out of Wonderland.
Joy meets elegance in delicately crafted jewelry treats.

ANNE ZELLIEN

Meaningful 'sentimental jewelry' – a style that was fashionable in Europe during the seventeenth and eighteenth centuries – has not fallen from use or lost desirability; it has even found contemporary expression in the hands of innovative designers, such as Anne Zellien. Anne has perfected the art of creating poetic yet lighthearted and playful keepsakes that renegotiate the traditional narratives of love and friendship. 'I would describe my jewelry as timeless but with a humorous twist,' she says. 'My *Messages* collection reached and inspired a lot of people, which made me very happy. But designing the *Vintage* collection is my favourite pastime – it makes me feel like a colt put out to pasture!' The *Messages* series fulfils a need for discreet and intimate amulets that we can invest with the powers to protect us. Short, uplifting mottos are engraved on – and sometimes concealed in – demure silver or gold compositions, as reminders that life is worth living. This buoyant spirit is carried over into the hedonistically themed *Vintage* collection, in which salvaged antique trinkets find a brand-new life and earrings are deliberately mismatched. It is a creative combustion in which the poetic resonance is offset by the use of precious charms that bring a sense of visual enchantment. 'Through my boutique in Antwerp, I can reach a greater audience with my collection and my bespoke work,' says Anne. 'Everything is produced in Belgium, the Netherlands and France. I can honestly say that I am currently experiencing the time of my life and the dream of a lifetime.' We can't help feeling that, like a benevolent friend, she must surely be infusing some of her own happiness into the creative formula.

www.annezellien.be

CLOCKWISE FROM LEFT

'Le Tapis Rouge' necklace of sterling silver and vintage parts, *Vintage* collection.

'Cloud 9' necklace of sterling silver and vintage parts, *Vintage* collection.

'How Much I Love You' earrings of sterling silver and vintage parts, *Vintage* collection.

BELOW 'Must Have' ring in 18kt yellow gold, *Du Bout du Fil* collection.

RIGHT 'It Girl' ring in 18kt yellow gold, with diamond, *Du Bout du Fil* collection.

ABOVE 'Vanités' cufflinks of rock crystal, mother of pearl and sterling silver bone.

LEFT 'Boulle' ring of ebony wood and 18kt yellow gold, *All in Wood* collection.

FAR LEFT 'Tank' ring of ebony wood and 18kt yellow gold, *All in Wood* collection.

BENEDIKT VON LEPEL

The witty use of wording in such rings as 'Must Have' and 'It Girl' is a nod to fashion fancy and a whispered concession to girlishness. The simplicity of Benedikt von Lepel's creations derives from brilliant miniaturism, pristine lines and an intoxicating lightness that only expert craftsmanship can deliver. Benedikt can trace her design curiosity back to her family's artistic leanings (her father is an art collector and her sister an antique jewelry collector), and for five years she herself worked as a contemporary art consultant. But the life-changing experience for the self-taught Benedikt was an encounter with a master jeweler, who invited her into his Parisian workshop and mentored her for over a year. 'I believe I am an artisan/designer,' she says, 'since my work revolves around innovative ideas yet is entirely handmade with traditional jewelers' tools.' Her chic *Doppia* collection is a prime example of this signature blend of modern ingenuity and airy preciousness. Thanks to a discreet mechanism, rings (adorned with semi-precious, faceted gems from Brazil) can be transformed into bracelets or pendant charms – chameleon-like, multi-purpose novelties. The same formula, but using bolder materials and with a focus on an ebony and gold combo, is used in the *All in Wood* collection, where elegance, polish and a hint of Art Deco are rolled into one. 'Travel, art, fashion … many things inspire me. But I have a particular interest in transforming functional daily objects into jewelry pieces,' Benedikt says. 'I also enjoy applying my creative drive to collaborations with other brands, exploring new territories. All aspects of the creative process fill me with joy. However, from the conception to the making, dealing with the material is what really enthrals me.' And us, too.

www.benediktvonlepel.com

CRISTINA ZAZO

Look closer. Cristina Zazo's elegant jewelry is punctuated by creatures from a dreamlike world with its own peculiar flora and fauna. Semi-precious stones are set tightly within the jaws of mythological skulls, while graceful orchids nestle semi-translucent gems cut *en cabochon* like precious drops of nectar. Perfect proportions, a delicious colour spectrum and the vitreous lustre of fluorite gems set against the warm tones of 18k gold-plating ensure a discreet luxury. 'As a child I had two passions: clay models and miniature things,' confides Cristina. 'I have reignited these early fascinations in my jewelry by bringing together sculptural elements and

attention to tiny detail.' Cristina studied fine arts at the Complutense University in Madrid but developed a passion for fashion design during her last year of study. After obtaining a Masters in accessories, she began to focus on jewelry design. While developing her own collections, she was also commissioned to create two per year exclusively for the Thyssen-Bornemisza Museum in Madrid. Today she occasionally collaborates with other local artisans, such as the Granja Royal Glass Factory in Segovia, which has supplied her with custom-pressed glass. She attributes her success to a mixture of hard work and creativity. 'I am always in a sort of attentive, steady mood; almost daydreaming. Every time something catches my attention or intrigues me, it fires off my inspiration and provides me with a thread to follow.' Her ideas are usually translated directly into wax carvings. She then works her magic until gold strikes, 'when I cannot stop looking at the final result'. Cristina's jewelry is a must-have for the kind of wearer who enjoys looking impeccable yet sensual; the kind of sleek, modern woman who is secretly tempted to get a tattoo.

www.cristinazazo.com

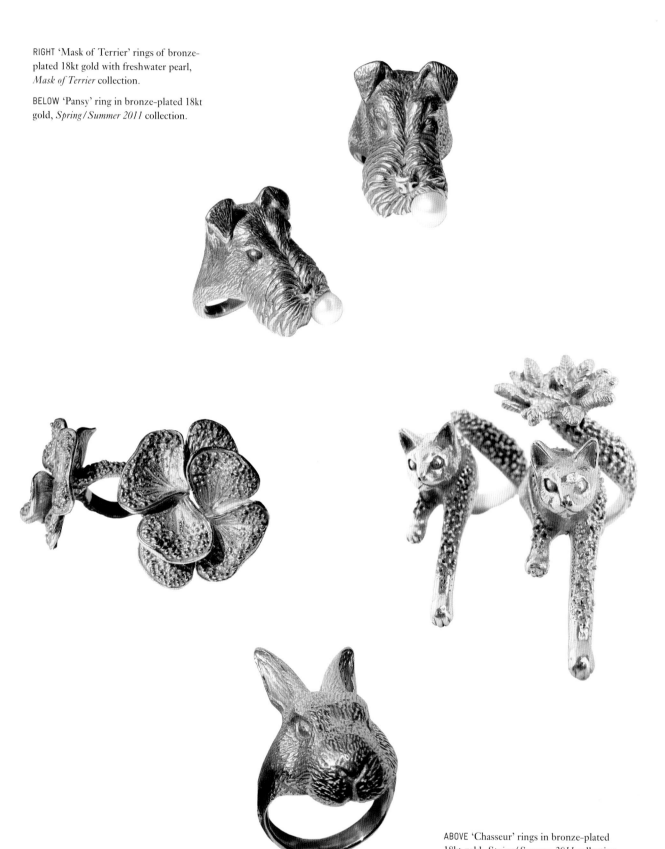

RIGHT 'Mask of Terrier' rings of bronze-plated 18kt gold with freshwater pearl, *Mask of Terrier* collection.

BELOW 'Pansy' ring in bronze-plated 18kt gold, *Spring/Summer 2011* collection.

ABOVE 'Chasseur' rings in bronze-plated 18kt gold, *Spring/Summer 2011* collection.

LEFT 'Mask of Rabbit' ring in bronze-plated 18kt gold, *Mask of Rabbit* collection.

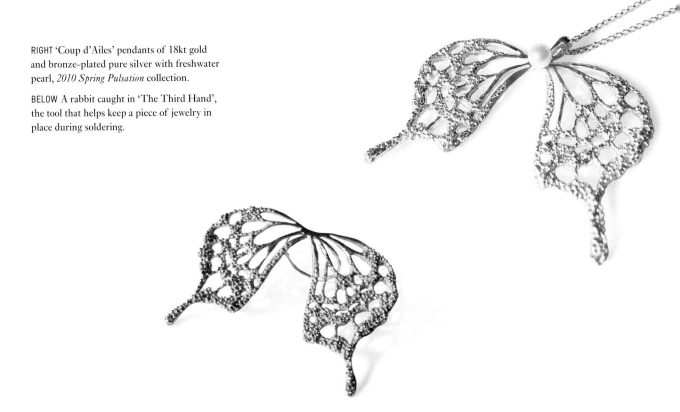

RIGHT 'Coup d'Ailes' pendants of 18kt gold and bronze-plated pure silver with freshwater pearl, *2010 Spring Pulsation* collection.

BELOW A rabbit caught in 'The Third Hand', the tool that helps keep a piece of jewelry in place during soldering.

CULOYON

'This morning a rabbit killed a hunter' ... the famous French children's song from the 1970s by Chantal Goya comes to mind when scrutinizing the menagerie of characters – rabbits, cats and terriers – that adorn the rings, earrings and pendants of the Japanese-born, Paris-based designer Yoshiko Parise. The surreal message of the French song, in which the hunting roles are reversed, is echoed in Culoyon's fairy-tale creations, which avoid cutesiness thanks to their sculptural poise and noble materials – silver, vermeil, bronze and gems. They seem to belong to surrealist cinematic narratives rather than to any other genre. Yoshiko revels in

translating the 'small worlds' that inhabit her imagination into drawings, which are then brought to life through sculpture. 'By creating jewelry, I like to tell stories,' she explains. 'It's probably due to the way I started working. I joined the Maison des Artistes, where I was primarily registered as an artist for wearable art.' She had already been creating fancy jewelry in her twenties back in Japan, but her life took a more artistic turn when she arrived in France and joined the BJOP school of jewelry. Her work seems happily to accommodate subtle influences from both Paris and Japan. 'The most exciting aspect of designing jewelry is that my imagination can flow freely,' Yoshiko says. 'Right now I'm designing jewelry that will capture the magnificence and fantasy of underwater flora and fauna.' A definite departure from her signature *Chasseur* series, this is perhaps the next logical step in a wondrous creative adventure. Who knows what fantastical creatures Yoshiko will drag up from her imaginary dive expeditions in Wonderland? No doubt they will resemble what Alice would have found had she fallen into a magical ocean hole.

www.culoyon.com

RIGHT 'Heaven Sent VIII' brooch of granulated Britannia silver, diamond, black diamond, yellow sapphire, tourmaline, peridot, smoky quartz and hessonite, *Heaven Sent* collection.

BELOW Organic meets geometric: inspirational images in Frances Wadsworth-Jones's East London studio.

FRANCES WADSWORTH-JONES

Parading their bulbous abdomens and fragile antennae, a pack of black ants seems determined to escape with a golden ring. This sculpturally evocative yet whimsical still life offers a sneak peek into an otherwise inaccessible microcosm. Frances Wadsworth-Jones sheds light on the mundane little aspects of our lives, orchestrating them into detailed and slightly surreal narratives. 'I love taking big ideas and playing them out on a small scale. People often have rigid ideas of what jewelry is, which means that it's much easier to take people by surprise,' she says. She revels in experimenting with anything technical, as long as it takes her

where she needs to be: from the combination of 3D computer modelling with traditional hand skills to create the minute detail of the *Workers* collection (in the installation piece 'Reel', a ten-metre-long chain at first appears to be machine-constructed but is in fact entirely handmade, with over 600 solders in one metre) to the ancient technique of granulation for the *Heaven Sent* collection (in which an ugly bird-dropping incident is transformed into a delightful adornment), or the industrial CNC wire-bending that she used to mass-produce the *Butterfly Clips* collection (in which worthless binder clips are remodelled into precious, metaphorical butterflies). 'I would describe my work as fine jewelry with a sense of humour – playing with the rules, and investigating that strange beauty that exists at the fine line between repulsion and seduction,' Frances says. 'I enjoy it when a man is brave enough to wear one of my pieces.' No need to taunt ... you have won us all over already.

www.franceswadsworthjones.com

RIGHT 'Thieves I' ring in stand: 18kt yellow gold and oxidized silver, *Workers* collection.

BELOW LEFT 'Thieves II' ring of 18kt yellow gold, and Tsavorite and white sapphires, *Workers* collection.

BELOW RIGHT 'Thieves VII' ring of 18kt yellow gold, oval sapphire and diamonds, *Workers* collection.

ABOVE 'Atlas Pin' brooch of 18kt yellow gold and Akoya pearl in handmade velvet-lined matchbox, *Workers* collection.

ABOVE RIGHT 'Jewel Thief' pendant of 18kt yellow gold and green tourmaline, *Workers* collection.

LEFT 'Winter' cuff of sterling silver, oxidized silver, 18kt yellow gold and pink sapphires.

BELOW CENTRE 'In Our Kitchen' ring of 18kt yellow gold, onyx and pearl.

BOTTOM LEFT 'Night Chameleon' ring of oxidized sterling silver, 18kt yellow gold, champagne diamonds and purple sapphires.

ABOVE 'Dove on a Walnut Branch' ring of sterling silver, oxidized silver, gold-plating, emeralds and rubies.

BELOW 'Celestial Goldfish' ring of 18kt yellow
gold and Swiss blue topazes.

RIGHT Like a teller of fairy tales: a peek inside
Manya Tessler's sketchbooks.

BOTTOM 'Garden Snail' ring of 18kt yellow gold,
oxidized sterling silver and pink sapphires.

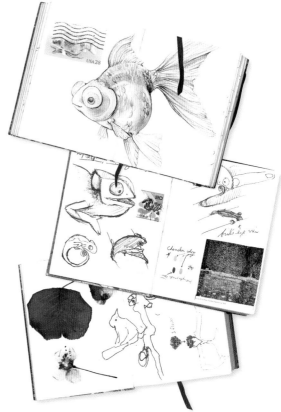

MANYA & ROUMEN

Manya & Roumen have elevated the art of sculptural jewelry
making to heavenly heights with their limited-edition hyper-
realistic animal rings. The Noah's Ark they have developed
is a treasure trove that feeds our inner child's sense of
wonder and our grown-up appreciation of luxury craft. The
gifted husband-and-wife team (Roumen Vragov is an info-
economics professor and Manya Tessler an artist/illustrator)
registered the company in 2009. 'The idea that I could be
a jewelry designer was planted by my wax-carving teacher,
Alan Brodsky, who treated us like professionals,' Manya
explains. 'With the encouragement of my husband, friends
and one very special uncle, I continued designing rings until
one day we realized that, with Roumen's business background and my passion for making jewelry, maybe this could
be our profession.' Rings wrap around a finger and therefore
lend themselves to 3D story-telling. Often filling entire
sketchbooks, Manya ends up benefiting from a plethora
of project-starters. Her work also allows her to honour
her affinity with the animal kingdom: 5% of the company's
profits is donated to animal charities. 'Once I started
making animal rings, I felt I had found my niche. I just love
making a little animal. It reminds me of the tiny toy eraser-
animals I used to play with,' she says. Be lulled by Manya

& Roumen's recycled yellow gold and rich black oxidized
silver, married with vibrant cabochons, faceted gems and
raw minerals. 'Each ring is like a chocolate bonbon: bite-
sized,' says Manya, smiling. Her wondrous materials are
skilfully morphed into charming companions that surely
have the power to ward off even a hint of a bad mood.

www.manyaandroumen.com

MARC ALARY

The renowned American ecologist Garrett Hardin once said: 'No one should be able to enter a wilderness by mechanical means.' Well, one intrepid explorer has done precisely that by crafting a utopian kingdom of exotic and ingeniously articulated wild animals. The result is fantastic, in every sense of the word. Marc Alary's work is a showcase of detailed artistry that breathes fresh, new, safari-scented air into the world of fine jewelry. The Toulouse-born designer began his career as an art director for music labels in Paris before moving to New York, where he freelanced for leading fashion brands such as DKNY, Louis Vuitton and Marc

Jacobs. 'I studied graphic design and fine arts, and worked as an illustrator before becoming more involved in fashion … until I got the bug for jewelry. Compared to illustration, I love the idea that you can hold this tiny object in your hands. It's like a portable perpetual reminder of a dream,' he says. 'I keep working in other fields, though, as I believe it helps me with my jewelry work – every form of art is connected.' Marc's debut collection, *Ménagerie*, satisfies our appreciation for innovative craft and sparks our curiosity: elephants, monkeys, panthers, zebras and flamingos roam mischievously around their newfound territory, the human body. 'I love gold for its versatility. You can texture it with different finishing and polishing,' Marc enthuses. 'I also love diamonds, as they come in so many cuts, sizes and colours; Padparadscha sapphires, which have sunset shades; and green, pink or Paraiba tourmalines.' Both *Ménagerie* and *Caravan* collections possess all the classic characteristics of exquisite fine jewelry, yet they have the ability to ignite a sense of pure joy, like that experienced by a child before a dazzling puppet show.

www.marcalary.com

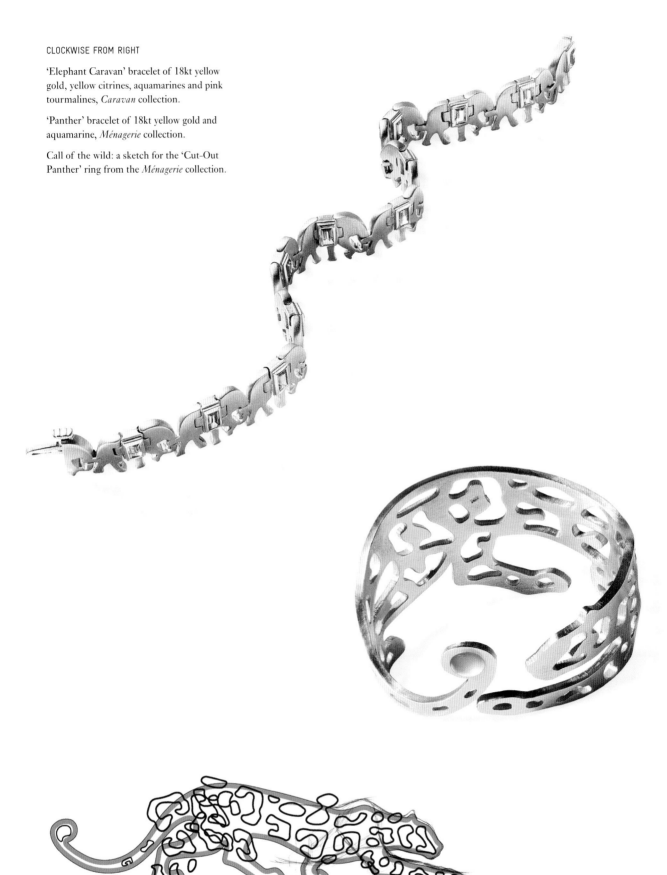

CLOCKWISE FROM RIGHT

'Elephant Caravan' bracelet of 18kt yellow gold, yellow citrines, aquamarines and pink tourmalines, *Caravan* collection.

'Panther' bracelet of 18kt yellow gold and aquamarine, *Ménagerie* collection.

Call of the wild: a sketch for the 'Cut-Out Panther' ring from the *Ménagerie* collection.

BELOW LEFT 'Spring' ring of 18kt white gold and green diamonds, *Four Seasons Ring* collection.

BELOW CENTRE 'Winter' ring of 18kt white gold and white diamonds, *Four Seasons Ring* collection.

FAR RIGHT 'Zebra Pavé' necklace of 18kt white gold, pavé black diamonds and black pearls, *Caravan* collection.

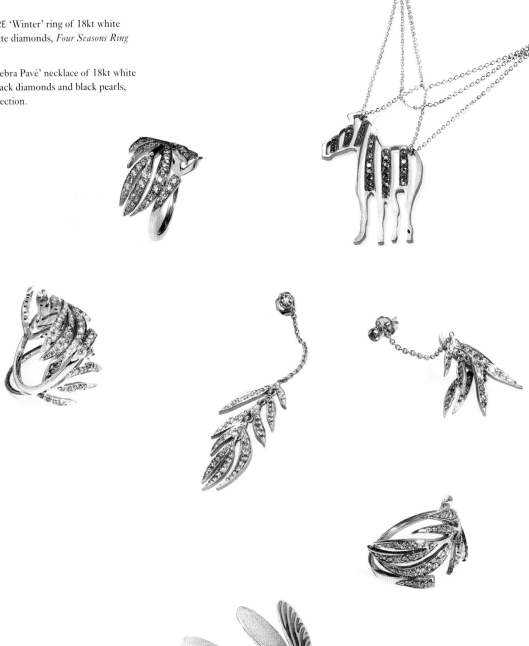

ABOVE RIGHT 'Full Leaf Pavé' earrings of 18kt yellow gold and pavé champagne diamonds, *Caravan* collection.

CENTRE RIGHT 'Fall' ring of 18kt yellow gold and champagne diamonds, *Four Seasons Ring* collection.

RIGHT 'Demoiselles' ring of 18kt white gold, pink and green tourmalines, and black enamel, *Caravan* collection.

CLOCKWISE FROM TOP LEFT

'Our Lady Of Guadalupe' necklace in 18kt gold-plated brass, *Saints* collection.

'Heart Flowers and Butterflies' necklace in 18kt gold-plated brass, *Hearts* collection.

'Match' of 18kt gold and enamel.

'Koi Fish' necklace in 18kt gold-plated brass, *Pop* collection.

OPPOSITE, CLOCKWISE FROM TOP LEFT

'Cristo Redentor' necklace in 18kt gold-plated brass, *Placês* collection.

'Coco Chanel' necklace of black obsidian, 18kt gold and pearls, *Skulls* collection.

Patricia Falcão in her colourful atelier.

PAT FALCÃO

Less painful and 'oh my god it's permanent' than a tattoo, more precious and sentimental than a stencil, Patricia Falcão's pendants of cut-out gold or silver (pure or in plated brass) are whimsical, witty and sexy picture-charms. Feeling pious? Jesus Christ or the Virgin Mary will embrace you with love. Getting romantic? Butterflies, hibiscus flowers and birds will set the mood. Looking for some edge? A grinning skull or a dashing koi carp will do the trick nicely. 'My pieces never go out of date – I just add new styles so I don't have to discharge them after every season – and if a piece isn't exactly as I have imagined, I recycle the metal and start again,' the Brazilian designer explains. Most of her narratives explore flora and fauna, religious imagery, skulls and Pop themes through intricate illustrations that Patricia then replicates in lace-like compositions. The chemical-cutting technique she uses to create her naturalistic imagery gives a deceptive fragility to the work – a skill that reflects her engineering background (she has an M.Sc. in Building Materials and Environmental Sciences from the University of São Paulo). 'I am passionate about drawing. Jewelry making is the best way I've found to materialize the drawings out of the paper,' she says. 'I research a lot of images, select the ones that reflect the mood I'm envisioning and start to

create my drawings, which will ultimately become a trinket.' Fuelled by a huge admiration for the works of both Andy Warhol (which lend humour and the Pop reference) and René Lalique (for the Art Nouveau flavour and discreet ostentation), Patricia has dreamt up a wonderfully cheerful oasis of sensual 'Brazilianity'.

www.patfalcao.com.br / http://patfalcao.blogspot.com

ABOVE 'Bumble Bee' necklace in 18kt yellow gold, with diamonds and Tsavorite eyes, *Ode to Artemis* collection.

BOTTOM Hand-finishing a moth with a piercing saw to enhance its details.

PHILIPPA HOLLAND

Delicate arachnids, bumblebees, beetles and butterflies join in a Darwinesque dance among seed-pods and leaves to create a charmingly nostalgic, yet sometimes creepy-crawly feel ... especially when a scorpion enters the scene. Entomology and botany don't get much more desirable than this. Philippa Holland's jewelry is anchored between graceful gentleness and feminine rock vibe. 'I feel like I'm wearing the woods when I wear my sycamore pod necklace,' she muses. 'It reminds me of my connection with nature.' Philippa describes herself as 'a bit of a gypsy', always on the move – horseriding whenever possible, and travelling in Romany-style caravans. She is constantly inspired, and revels above all in the research phase of her work. 'I favour diamonds – in all colours. However, I also use other gems and beads. It all started when I strung them into necklaces or set them in gold, which organically led to experimenting with electro-forming and casting from natural findings, thereby defining my creative signature,' she explains. All her pieces are manufactured in England by skilled craftsmen, ensuring high-quality creations that surpass their fashion credentials to become gorgeous family heirlooms. Some of the gold is panned in Australia, which is about as eco-friendly as you can get when it comes to obtaining non-recycled gold; gems are sourced in Jaipur, India. 'Depending on the collection,' says Philippa, 'we have some pieces that sell to high-end fashionistas and some that are bought for traditional special occasions, such as weddings or christenings.' By reconnecting us to the realm of living things and sprinkling subtle references to the spirit world, Philippa allegorizes the relationship between nature and jewelry. Gems glitter, naturalistic wonders abound; it is as if we have stepped into a modern-day fairyland.

www.philippaholland.co.uk

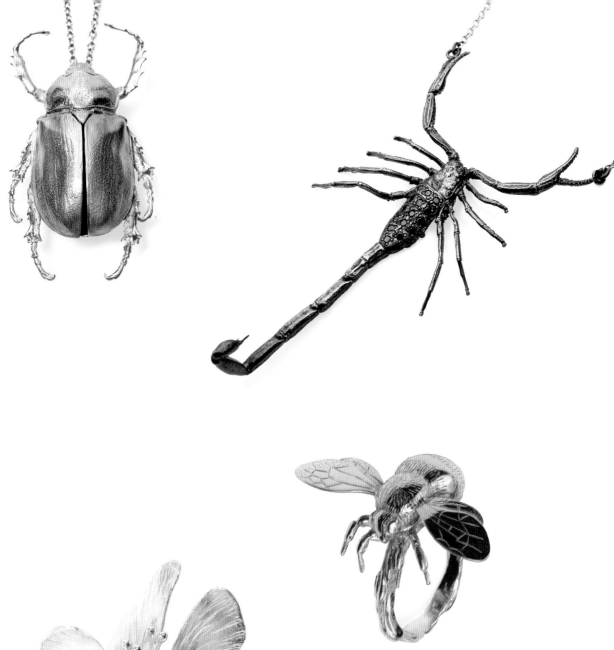

CLOCKWISE FROM TOP LEFT

'Beetle' necklace of silver, 24kt gold plate and enamel, *Ode to Artemis* collection.

'Scorpion' necklace in blackened silver, with Tsavorite eyes, *Nature's Tricks* collection.

'Bumble Bee' ring of 9kt yellow gold and diamonds, with Tsavorite eyes, *Ode to Artemis* collection.

'Moth in Motion' ring of silver, 24kt gold plate and diamonds, *Ode to Artemis* collection.

'Sycamore Pod' ring of 9kt yellow gold, *English Folk* collection.

'Twig' rings of yellow, rose and white 18kt gold, with diamonds, *English Folk* collection.

'Eye' ring of 18kt yellow gold, onyx and pink tourmalines, *Cocktail Rings* collection.

BELOW Devilish freshwater pearls with custom-cut semi-precious stones, *Punk Pearl* collection.

BOTTOM 'Kitten' ring of 18kt gold and freshwater pearl, with tourmaline ears, *Punk Pearl* collection.

SABINA KASPER

One day, while walking alone admiring the raw force and beauty of nature on the 'Glacière' footpath to Mont Blanc, Sabina Kasper had an epiphany: she would quit her economics and law studies to embark on a new, creative path. Soon afterwards she enrolled at the Swedish Konstfack College of Arts, Crafts and Design. She also took the opportunity to spend six months at Tohoku Art University in Japan, where she mastered ancient metalsmithing tech-

niques. Eager to keep travelling, she went to São Paulo to create the accessory line for avant-garde Brazilian designer Gloria Coelho. Back in Sweden, in 2005, she finally launched her own brand, using both traditional craft and groundbreaking experimental techniques to apply industrial procedures to precious materials. Think laser-printed freshwater pearls, 925 silver chains coated with fluorescent neon polyamide paint, and tourmaline hand-painted with industrial lacquer for a techno girly vibe. The result is a highly unusual and joyful collection of precious, delicious showstoppers; whimsy brought to a whole new level of innovation and desirability. Sabina, a self-proclaimed *enfant terrible*, sums up why she is so passionate about jewelry: 'The magic, the customized storytelling, the eternity, and the energy from light, colours, weight and patina.' She is currently embracing a 'less is more' approach, which has been a hit with style hunters and the trendiest stores – Dover Street and Liberty in London, Colette in Paris, Octium in Kuwait, Acne Jeans worldwide. Gratifying as success is, it also dictates a hectic pace: 'Sometimes it's just too challenging; it feels like a concentrated chaos,' says Sabina, 'but paradoxically I wouldn't trade it for anything else.' Luckily for us.

www.sabinakasper.com

BELOW 'Paint' hook earrings in 18kt gold with hand-painted tourmaline, *Paint* collection.

RIGHT 'Paint' chain earring in 18kt gold with hand-painted tourmaline, *Paint* collection.

ABOVE RIGHT 'Paint' pin brooch in 18kt gold with hand-painted tourmaline, *Paint* collection.

RIGHT 'Paint' bracelet in 18kt gold with hand-painted tourmaline, *Paint* collection.

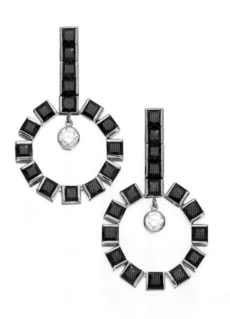

'Sunflower' earrings in 22kt yellow gold and diamonds, *Collection 1*.

'Small Blessing' necklace of 18kt blackened rhodium white gold, 18kt yellow gold, AA South Sea and Tahitian pearls, enamel and diamonds, *Collection 3*.

'Ruby' earrings of 18kt yellow gold, rubies and diamonds, *Collection 1*.

'Maze' ring of 18kt yellow gold, rubies and pearls, *Collection 1*.

STEPHANIE SIMON

There is one school of sculptural jewelry in which the style is monolithic and angular, and another in which roundness and playfulness are at work. Stephanie Simon's jewelry belongs to the latter. Her collections, which pair poetic ingenuity with luxurious quirkiness, are built around gold ('for the intensity of the colour'), diamonds, pearls and coloured gems ('thrown in for good measure'). All have an equal place in Stephanie's heart. Look at her *Collection 1* and fantasize about endless summers with the 22kt gold petals that cluster round a 1.51ct solitaire in the 'Sunflower' ring, or express your understated glamour as you tuck your hair

behind your ear to reveal glorious 'Ruby' earrings. *Collection 2* is a witty nod to one's inner teenager and reflects a longing to love, dance and laugh, as in the 'Rave' ring of gold and bright yellow enamel. *Collection 3* steps into rock/goth terrain with the sleek '4 Cross' rings and 'Small Blessing' earrings and necklace, a contemporary take on rosaries and religious keepsakes. Growing up in Trinidad, where jewelry is adored, London-based Stephanie has been fascinated by the 'endless possibilities' that jewelry provides for as long as she can remember. Launching her own line was therefore 'a natural progression', she says. 'The moment the inspiration translates to the actual piece is immensely rewarding. The interest to me is the idea and the end process.' Stephanie's approach speaks to individuals who are confident, stylish and have a sense of humour. Scenesters or the jaded should go their own way.

www.stephaniesimon.co.uk

ABOVE LEFT '4 Cross' ring of 18kt yellow gold, with red enamel, *Collection 3*.

ABOVE Stephanie Simon assessing a diamond for quality.

LEFT 'Sunflower' ring in 22kt yellow gold and diamond, *Collection 1*.

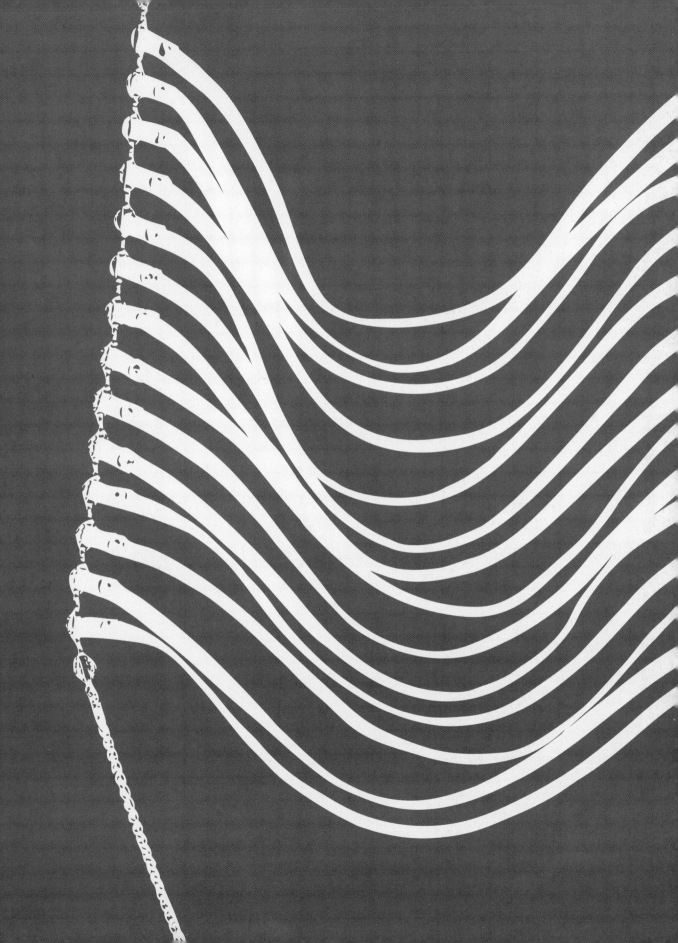

THE HIP PACK

Edgy jewelry for the tribe of the effortlessly cool.
Now you have the code.

ANNIE COSTELLO BROWN

It is probably thanks to her unconventional upbringing on Californian houseboats, raised by two creative parents and surrounded by adults who made their own fashion, art and music, that Annie Costello Brown has developed such a forceful artistic drive, even now inspired by those hand-crafts of the 1960s and '70s. 'When I cried like any typical 13-year-old girl because I couldn't have the designer clothes I wanted, my mom said, "Necessity is the mother of invention", and that I needed to be cool to survive,' she exclaims. A life lesson in resourcefulness. With the loyal fan-base that her edgy, urban, tribalistic collections have earned, Annie has positioned her forward-thinking creations beyond cool. Former Yves Saint Laurent designer Stefano Pilati swooped in, inviting her to collaborate on their *Edition 24* line – possibly the most confidence-boosting experience in Annie's career. Despite her success, she has kept all design and production processes in her Los Angeles studio, where she constantly experiments with new combinations. 'My obsession to change aesthetics and my deep yet infantile need to find uniquity dictate how I design jewelry,' she explains. Her work is focused on using innovative techniques and approaches to glorify humble rather than precious materials – stones, beads, leather, brass and bronze, for example – and on ensuring desirability. 'I'm not fancy or girly at all. I prefer jewelry, clothes and household objects to have character and quality rather than be a logo,' she states. And when asked about her professional ambitions, her down-to-earth acumen shines through, as she replies that she has chosen the '"slow and steady wins the race" business model!'

http://anniecostellobrown.com

'Black Linea Blades' necklace of leather-covered chain, dyed cotton rope, brass beads and black-dipped bronze castings.

'Dione' necklace of vintage brass chain and beads, shell and African vinyl beads.

'Quiddiem' necklace of patina brass, vintage brass chain, leather and bronze castings.

OPPOSITE, CLOCKWISE FROM TOP LEFT

'Face Veil' in silver chains.

'Diamond Pavé Nail' ring of 14kt yellow gold and diamonds, with ruby eyes, *Serpensive* collection.

'Pavé Birdskull Nail' ring of 14kt yellow gold, with ruby eyes and black diamond crown, *Scream and Spirit* collection, made exclusively for the 'Keep a Child Alive' organization.

'Fool's Gold' bangle of 14kt yellow gold and pyrite, *Rock* collection.

BELOW Sketch showing concepts for the *Seize Kind* collection, including a development of Jules Kim's signature 'single-finger fit, multi-finger look' bar ring.

BOTTOM 'Fairy Duster' ring of 14kt gold and pavé diamonds, *Rock* collection.

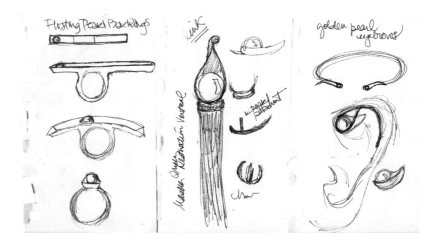

BIJULES

A jewelry luminary, whose hybrid modernist creations have become the addiction of many famous (and not-so-famous) fashionistas, Jules Kim is perpetually rethinking the boundaries between art, fashion and luxury … all the while keeping a keen eye on the zeitgeist. Her thought-provoking ideas come from myriad sources: from found materials in nature, such as mouse bones and raw minerals, to children's toys, travel and the lives of people following a similar path. Around 2004, Jules, a.k.a. Bijules, realized that being audaciously creative was her calling. After graduating a crash course in Jewelry 101 at university, she set about challenging the fashion world's take on the concept of jewelry, thereby foiling the status quo. 'I adore the fact that I can push existing boundaries in several industries. I make storytelling pieces in fine metals, which stuns the luxury world but also makes them expand their own perception of what jewelry is,' she enthuses. 'To be successful I feel there are limitations that must be challenged and, as Andy Warhol once said, "Things couldn't look this strange and new without some barrier being broken."' Bijules fans seek the unconventional and invest considerable energy into researching interesting pieces and discovering how they relate to them. 'Passion is inherent in everything I do,' says Jules. 'When I have an idea it's extremely difficult to avoid manufacturing it. My design spirit is like a child who is constantly making mistakes, learning from them, and moving on. I try to develop new ways to communicate my artwork each season, each time.' Working with the coolest set – or, as she puts it, 'the best roster of media/entertainment/fashion people in the world' – Jules creates only a handful of models in order to develop a story that is unique to the collection; a story often tinged with irony, humour and empowering enchantment.

www.bijulesnyc.com

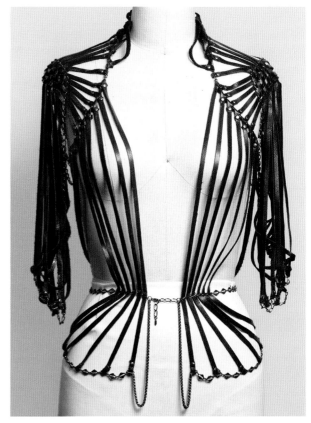

OPPOSITE ABOVE LEFT 'Boundary' jumper of slate-gray bovine leather and copper chain, *Embraced* collection.

OPPOSITE ABOVE RIGHT AND BELOW LEFT 'Gesture' skirt (worn as a dress) in black bovine leather with chain hem, *Embraced* collection.

OPPOSITE BELOW RIGHT 'Contour' jacket in bovine leather, with chain, *Embraced* collection.

RIGHT 'Riot' bracelet armband in bovine leather with hematite-plated disc bracelets and wrist cuff, *Signature* collection.

FAR RIGHT 'Killjoy' vest in bovine leather and chain, to be worn multiple ways, *Signature* collection.

BELOW Bliss Lau's design studio on Fifth Avenue, with mounted jewelry framed by strips of tape and a mock-up of a dress created for the Museum of Arts and Design.

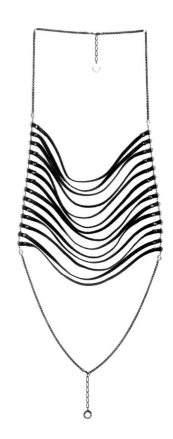

BLISS LAU

Redefining the boundaries between jewelry and apparel, leather straps and metal chains become, according to their designer, 'a decorative structure that hangs on the body to enhance its form'. In these fluid corset bones, these structural delimitations of an invisible uniform, there is a nod to costumes from the Roaring Twenties as well as a distinctly avant-garde vibe. Hawaii-raised Bliss Lau, a graduate of Parsons in New York, launched her first collection as a handbag designer. Some years later, for fun, she draped a handbag chain over a mannequin, thus creating her first body chain. Thereafter she focused on jewelry. 'I find working with

leather endlessly inspiring; silver and gold as well. In liquid form they can be modelled into any shape, as chains they can drape, and when solid they can hold a hard shape. The possibilities are endless,' she marvels. No surprises that Bliss's inspiration comes from 3D structures, be it Houdini's weathered straitjacket or a majestic waterfall. Her creative process involves three stages: sketching to draping, leatherworking, and back to sketching (although the order often changes). 'Each collection satisfies a new urge and gives a different kind of pleasure. Discovering new materials is always a highlight of the design process.' The *Mysterious Concealment* fine jewelry collection allowed Bliss to work directly on the skin, 'a fantastic design challenge', whereas the *Embraced* collection translated jewelry as coverings for the body, challenging its movement. According to Bliss, the people who wear her designs 'have no age because they don't care how old they are. They have no weight. They may or may not own a pair of heels, but they do have a very strong sense of themselves and are fearless when it comes to that.' And if you do not feel very fearless, simply trust that Bliss's urban feminine armour will reveal your hidden fierceness once you try it.

http://blisslau.com

RIGHT Not a private museum of natural history, but Julia deVille's intriguing workshop, stuffed with taxidermy works as well as fashion and jewelry creations.

BELOW 'Lily Rook' necklace of sterling silver, black rhodium and gold plate.

OPPOSITE, CLOCKWISE FROM TOP LEFT

'Bird Wing' brooch of pigeon wing and sterling silver.

'Lily Rosary' earrings of 18kt white gold, black diamonds and green quartz.

'Tangled Lily' necklace of sterling silver and gold plate.

'Actaeon' sculpture with stillborn deer, smoky quartz, sterling silver, chainmail and sparrow wings.

JULIA DEVILLE

Under Julia deVille's guidance, memento mori ('remember your mortality') no longer inspire dread or macabre thoughts. Her dark yet sentimentalized creations – jewelry and taxidermy go hand in hand – populate a beguiling theatre overflowing with curiosities; a place where past and present co-exist via references to Victoriana and futuristic fetishism. 'I want to inspire people to contemplate their own mortality, in a positive way. I'm not a morbid person, but I'm not afraid of acknowledging that I'm mortal,' states Julia. Using recycled materials whenever possible, the New Zealand-born, Melbourne-based designer dissects antique

jewelry to salvage stones and metals. 'I don't design things. I generally have a material – an animal, a stone – and from that I know what to make. It's a very organic, free process,' she says. With a passion for anything with a history, Julia favours what she tenderly calls 'my animals'. They are 'more precious to me than any gemstone and participate to my non-wearable, one-off, sculptural work. Of course, I go off on a tangent and make slightly prettier wearable things that are still within my style.' Her taxidermy characters are frozen in unexpected poses and variously adorned, although not anthropomorphized. 'They are little talismans that hold magical powers. Each one has a personality and I become very attached. I never want to sell them, but I do because I need to make a living,' she laughs. Julia addresses death as a universal concern and, via totemic artworks and a rock-chic vibe, seems to free it from taboo. Her *Disce Mori* ('Learn to Die') designs strike a chord with young goth kids and wealthy, conservative, older women alike ... and almost everyone in between.

http://juliadeville.com

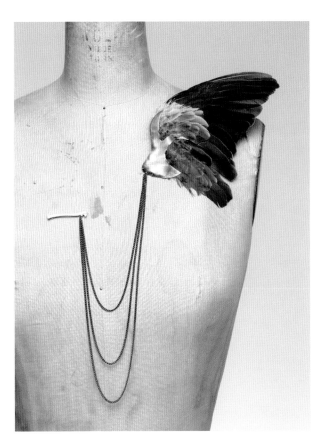

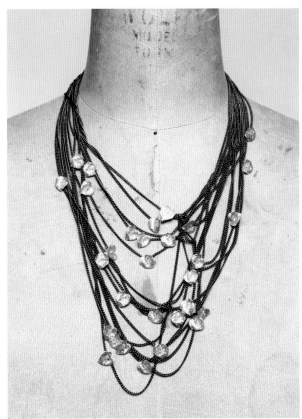

CLOCKWISE FROM RIGHT

'Calvinism' cufflinks of sterling silver and black rhodium plate.

'Emerald City' ring of 18kt white gold and emeralds.

'Death' ring of sterling silver and cubic zirconia.

'Death' cufflinks in blackened sterling silver.

'Funeral' ring in 9kt white gold, with garnet.

OPPOSITE 'Calvinism' large necklace in sterling silver.

CLOCKWISE FROM LEFT

'Heka Collar' necklace of antiqued bronze and crushed jet, *Fangs of Bastet* collection.

'Fringe Wing Collar' necklace of antiqued gunmetal and crushed jet, with ombré brass chain fringe, *Fangs of Bastet* collection.

'Arrow' cuff in antiqued bronze, *Fangs of Bastet* collection.

'Three Ring' cuff in antiqued bronze, *Fangs of Bastet* collection.

'Spear' ring of antiqued bronze and crushed jet, *Fangs of Bastet* collection.

RIGHT 'Heart' choker of antiqued gunmetal, crushed pyrite and jet, *Fangs of Bastet* collection.

BELOW 'Reflected Heart' ring of antiqued bronze, crushed pyrite and jet, *Fangs of Bastet* collection.

BOTTOM Jill Martinelli and Sabine Le Guyader working on production for their Fall 2011 deliveries.

LADY GREY

Next time you sit terrified in a dentist's chair, hold this thought from Jill Martinelli and Sabine Le Guyader, the creators of Lady Grey: 'The techniques and tools involved in dentistry are very similar to those used by a jeweler – a realization that triggered what would become our passion, when as teenagers we both had experience working in orthodontics.' Having studied sculpture and metalsmithing at Massachusetts College of Art, Jill and Sabine discovered a common interest in conceptual art, which accounts for their success in elevating body ornamentation beyond the realm of mere decoration. Add a dose of scientific curiosity and you get an inquisitive yet sensual trendsetting scenario. 'We love re-contextualizing traditional materials, so any material we can really manipulate is an instant favourite,' the duo explain. 'Right now we're into crushing semi-precious stones that we set in our own handcrafted bezels of various shapes. Every day is like science class in our studio!' A new and shrewd take on cabochon setting is at the centre of their futuristically edgy *Fangs of Bastet* collection, an ode to Egyptian mythology and ancient symbolism. Vulture wings and scarabs are revisited using cast bronze spikes adorned with crushed pyrite and jet, finished in either antiqued brass or antiqued gunmetal plating to give a mysterious touch of the past. From their debut collection, inspired by the theme of decay, to the *Fangs of Bastet*, Lady Grey has remained committed to subverting standard concepts of beauty by transforming macabre objects into desirable fashion items. Their exhilarating, unorthodox jewelry is at the vanguard of an aesthetic revolution.

www.ladygreyjewelry.com

LEFT 'She's Dead' cuff in trimming, brass and black metal.

BELOW Shall the creatures of night rise: Frédéric Baldo and Ludivine Machinet.

BOTTOM 'True Devotion' bracelet of white gold metal, and black and pale pink enamel.

NUIT N°12

Masked spectres from the underside of life, ghostly envoys of the occult night, and ultimately the tempter – the winged beast – emerging from the shadows to emanate an intoxicating sensuality. The spirit of the phantom of the opera hovers over the darkly sexy gewgaws of Nuit N°12, the brainchild of French designers Ludivine Machinet and Frédéric Baldo. 'Transgressing the borders of jewelry creation is our aim. All our pieces are objects of curiosity, rare and fantastic, opulent and symbolic, fashioned with highly skilled craft,' they say. 'They awaken the senses, trigger a devouring obsession, and become talismanic.' It is this powerful narrative that informs Nuit N°12's creations. With complex techniques and experimentation, and with the help of scores of skilled artisans, they constantly test the limits of jewelry design. Brass, wood and Plexiglas are combined, then lacquered or enamelled for a flawless lustre that oozes gothic glamour. As for the dream palette for catacomb wraiths, black is a given, then silver for shining armour and dusty pink for haunting seduction. It is during the night that 'reality is banished from the dream world' and lust is playfully fetishized. According to the design duo, 'Our muse is a hybrid creature, somewhere between Anita Berber, Medea and Simonetta Gianfelici.' Perhaps a style-conscious night-and-day bird, for whom fashion jewelry is a swanky, totemic essential? Ludivine and Frédéric's dream for the future is to expand Nuit N°12 beyond fashion accessories by developing ready-to-wear lines, cosmetics and product designs – ultimately, to build an all-inclusive lifestyle brand. And when that moment comes, hallelujah! The elusive forces of the night will storm our daylight hours.

www.nuitnumero12.com

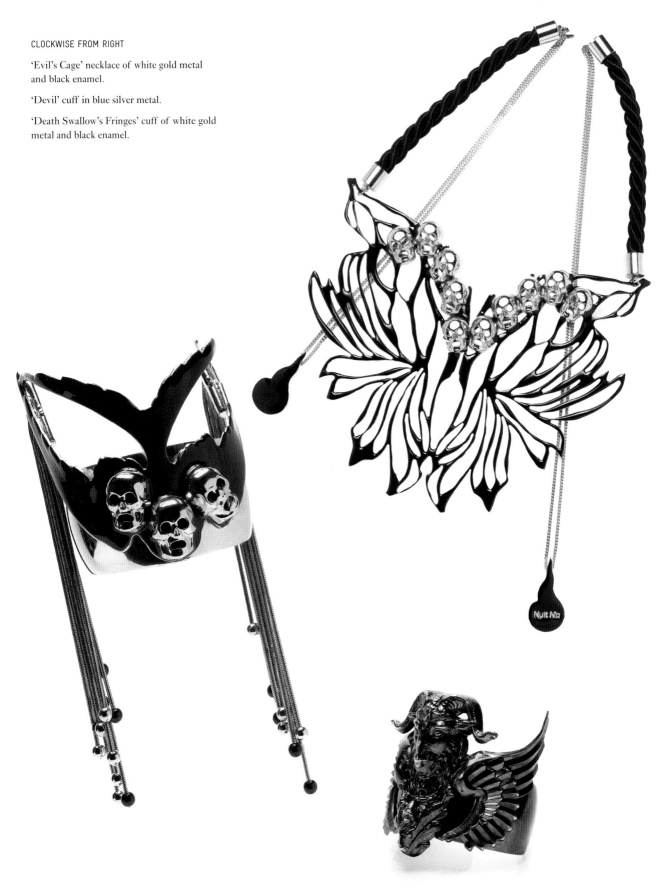

CLOCKWISE FROM RIGHT

'Evil's Cage' necklace of white gold metal and black enamel.

'Devil' cuff in blue silver metal.

'Death Swallow's Fringes' cuff of white gold metal and black enamel.

RIGHT Necklace of turtle bone, pyrite and calcite.

BELOW Regina Dabdab's shamanistic creations displayed on branches in her studio, like dream-catchers.

OPPOSITE, CLOCKWISE FROM TOP LEFT

Still life with rabbit, including a necklace of driftwood, coral and green tourmaline, a bracelet of teak wood and black tourmaline, and a bracelet of teak wood and pyrite.

'Graphical Composition 3' brooch of teak wood and Plexiglas.

Still life with crocodile, including a necklace of driftwood and pyrite.

Necklace of teak wood.

REGINA DABDAB

Nurturing a dazzling sense of *mise en scène*, Regina Dabdab constantly ups the style stakes when it comes to the display of her creations. She set her Constructivist-inspired first collection, with its graphic compositions in acrylic and wood marquetry, against a simple, pitch-black background. For her part-geological, part-statuesque second collection – an organic, match-made-in-heaven pairing of raw semi-precious stones with driftwood, coral, horn, bones and other exotic finds – she created an opulent, still-life backdrop in the style of the old Flemish masters, thereby blurring our perceptions of time. Perhaps carbon-dating would reveal

whether Regina's Stone Age-looking emblems precede (as ritualistic remnants from an ancient civilization) or post-date (as meteoric messengers from a futuristic or alien society) the intriguing props used in their display. Based in Paris, Regina is a Brazilian accessories designer who graduated from the Faculdade Santa Marcelina in São Paulo, then specialized in accessories in Milan before attending Studio Berçot in Paris. 'My grandfather owned a stone shop in São Paulo, so I grew up among gems and semi-precious stones. I was always very excited to discover the variety of shapes, textures and colours, and this is certainly why they are my favourite materials to create from, especially pyrite,' she explains. 'I start by collecting my organic materials, then I work a composition by assembling them together. It comes quite naturally to me, as I feel that some of them genuinely have some connection potential with each other.' It is this responsiveness to natural laws that makes Regina's projects all the more eye-catching … and hotly anticipated.

http://reginadabdab.com

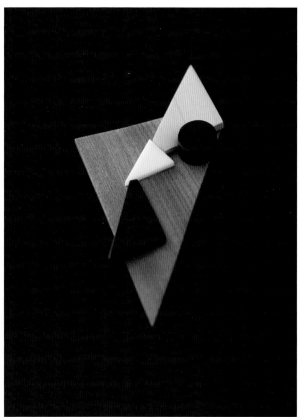

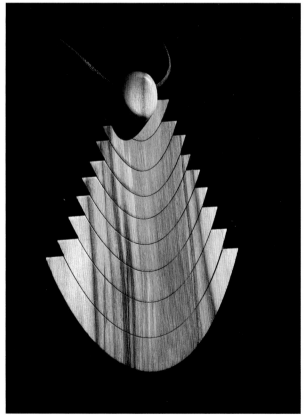

CLOCKWISE FROM RIGHT

'Pigeon Wing' headdress in metal–tipped leather, *V/ermin* collection.

'White Rat Bow Tie' neckpiece in leather, *V/ermin* collection.

'Pigeon Feather' cufflinks in sterling silver, *P/ark* collection.

'Fox Jaw' necklace in 18kt gold–plated silver, with sterling silver chain and leather strap, *P/ark* collection.

RIGHT Reid Peppard's studio and ossuary:
a quirky yet harmonious ensemble of props
and objects.

BELOW RIGHT 'Carrion Crow Talon'
pendants in 18kt gold-plated silver and in
sterling silver, with sterling silver chains,
P/ark collection.

RP/ENCORE

Channel your inner Hermes, messenger of the gods, by wearing a striking headpiece made of birds' wings. RP/Encore's regal accessories are directly cast or made from creatures such as carrion crows, grey squirrels and red foxes, reconnecting us with urban wildlife and reminding us of folk tales. These ethical taxidermy artworks (some are included in the Greenberg and Schwarz collections) are the brainchild of Reid Peppard, a member of the UK Guild of Taxidermists and a graduate of Central St Martins. Los Angeles-born Reid is now resident in London, where her studio is based and where her 'already dead' animals are scavenged. 'A lot of my work addresses issues I see in our treatment of the environment,' she notes. 'That's why I keep things small and handmade, and don't use carcinogenic chemicals such as Formalin.' Reid ensures her artifacts are durable by test-wearing them for at least a month. 'I love working with fur and feathers,' she enthuses, 'as well as with gold and sterling silver, whose natural antimicrobial properties are key.' Sketching is usually the starting point, followed by an experimental phase charged with technical challenges. 'My work is very organic and ritualistic in nature, so trial and error are an integral part of the process. Casting organs isn't easy. Making a crow clutch that actually works as a clutch and still looks like a crow is fairly difficult.' Reid's jewelry is cast in London's jewelry district, Hatton Garden, and is then brought to the studio to be hand-filed, polished and soldered before going to an assay office, where it receives UK hallmarks and its maker's mark, 'RP E'. Fantastic vehicles for self-expression (Lady Gaga and Sienna Miller agree), each anatomically precise amulet casts a little spell of its own.

www.rpencore.com

BELOW 'Heart' necklace in 925 silver, with bronze veins and leather lacing, oxidized and roughly polished.

BOTTOM Old punch sets found at flea markets used for hammering words into jewelry.

OPPOSITE, FROM TOP

'Antique Half' bangle in 925 silver, with bronze and copper mini skulls, stained oxidation.

'Leather Metal Braid' bracelet in 925 silver, pieces laced together with cotton and braided with leather cord.

'Skull Bead' double bracelet in black cotton cord macramé, with skull beads of two different sizes in 925 silver, bronze and copper.

'Silver Bar' double-wrap bracelet in 925 silver, with matt onyx beads, black tiger's eye beads and cotton cord.

TOBIAS WISTISEN

When Mad Max meets Danish Vikings, chaos could ensue. But, unexpectedly, the two unite in a rough and somewhat sinister yet refined urban-warrior decorum. We have entered the world of masculine accessories and blacksmithed jewelry. Born in Denmark and trained at ESMOD (École Supérieure des Arts et Techniques de la Mode) in Paris, Tobias Wistisen's first experience of the design industry was in the studio of John Galliano. 'I was working in fashion menswear, and the jewelry was one of the last things in the design process. As I got more and more in charge of the accessories, I realized that jewelry was much more fun than clothing. A no brainer: I quit and started my own label.' Key to Tobias's feudal and dark paradigm, which has already captured fashion editors, power players and would-be adventurers, is his relentless pursuit of the best possible outcome. 'I do tests for new braiding techniques, texture, colours and materials that I might want to use. I then start carving out the first waxes for the new pieces. When I have them in silver, I can try to assemble the finished jewelry and see how it looks. And then I pretty much change everything, because I've been looking at the drawings for a month and want something new!' Tobias recounts. 'Until the final presentation I carve and draw simultaneously, in order to get the best and most developed pieces in the collection.' Primal materials that connect with modern cool hunters – such as silver, crocodile, stingray and leather – are interwoven, sculpted and soldered into anarchistic yet controlled pieces of jewelry that look like war trophies. Battle for the best look, without question.

www.tobiaswistisen.com

RIGHT 'Multiple Shrunken Heads' necklace in 925 silver, six small shrunken heads with eyes and mouth laced together, hair of mini curb chain.

BELOW 'Drama' loop hanger for a belt hook or bag in 925 silver, with calf leather and horse teeth.

ABOVE 'Starburst' and 'Multiple Cross' rings in 925 silver, with bronze crosses.

LEFT 'Old Boot' necklace in 925 silver, with bronze skull, copper sole and heel riveted with silver nails, and cotton cord, rough stained oxidation.

LEFT 'Skull Crocodile' wallet chain, with eight crocodile fins set into 925 silver, tassel of calf leather.

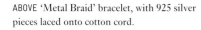

ABOVE 'Metal Braid' bracelet, with 925 silver pieces laced onto cotton cord.

RIGHT 'Riveted' ring in 925 silver, with cat's eye and ebony wood.

BELOW 'Large Prism' rings of 14kt gold and clear quartz prisms.

BOTTOM Cluster of 'Large Prism' and 'Mini Prism' rings of oxidized silver, 14kt gold vermeil and rose gold vermeil, clear quartz, smoky quartz, amethyst and black onyx prisms.

BELOW RIGHT 'AC/UN Collaboration' vial necklaces: 'Compost' with 14kt gold top and nude cord chain, and 'Blue Holi Colour' with sterling silver top and chain.

BOTTOM RIGHT 'Mini Prism' rings of oxidized silver, 14kt gold vermeil, rose gold vermeil and clear quartz prisms.

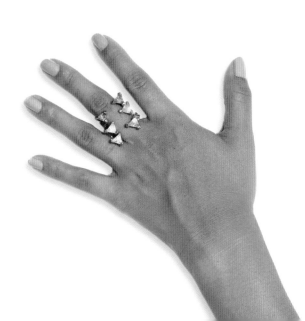

RIGHT 'Classic Crystal' pendants in bungee cord chain and a range of crystals – aqua aura quartz, titanium quartz, phantom quartz, amethyst, pyrite, clear quartz and green tourmaline.

BELOW Gia Bahm assembling her talismanic pieces at the studio bench.

UNEARTHEN

Phylactery has a new heroine: a fashion trailblazer who is so in tune with natural elements that she has encapsulated their therapeutic and spiritual properties in stylish urban adornments. At the heart of her amulets lies a duality: exquisite crystals are nested in empty bullet cases (healing versus destruction, birth versus death), in an elegiac bid to rebalance the earth's paradoxical forces. New York-based Gia Bahm is Unearthen's creator: 'I feel happiest when I am enveloped in the new worlds I can create through making jewelry collections. I am an independent worker and I couldn't help but only want to work with the natural elements of the world and

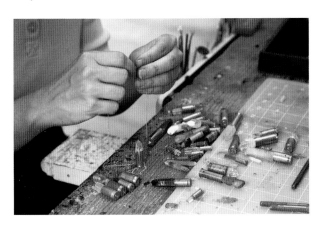

create something specific from them,' she claims. 'There's something so special and classic about a clear quartz, and there are beautiful blue tones of aquamarine, greens and pinks of tourmaline, that work brilliantly well with the tones of gold.' A modular array of crystals, carefully selected for their inherent holistic qualities, targets specific needs. As Gia notes, the crystals may help to 'clear your mind, focus your heart on goals you struggle to achieve, or provide comfort in difficult times'. The connection to the earth is even more exalted in her vial necklace series, where the list of ingredients reads like a geological/travel/magical potion brochure. Compost, crude oil, sand and water from the Pacific Ocean are the unorthodox keepsakes that somehow resonate with Gia's own unconventional self-description as a person with 'a somewhat detached manner', who is 'a seeker of authenticity; intuitive, sentimental, spontaneous and a promoter of personal freedom'. Alongside her pendant collections, Gia has designed rings, watches and cuffs that share the same design signatures – an esoteric ensemble, like futuristic relics of a super-civilization.

www.seeunearthen.com

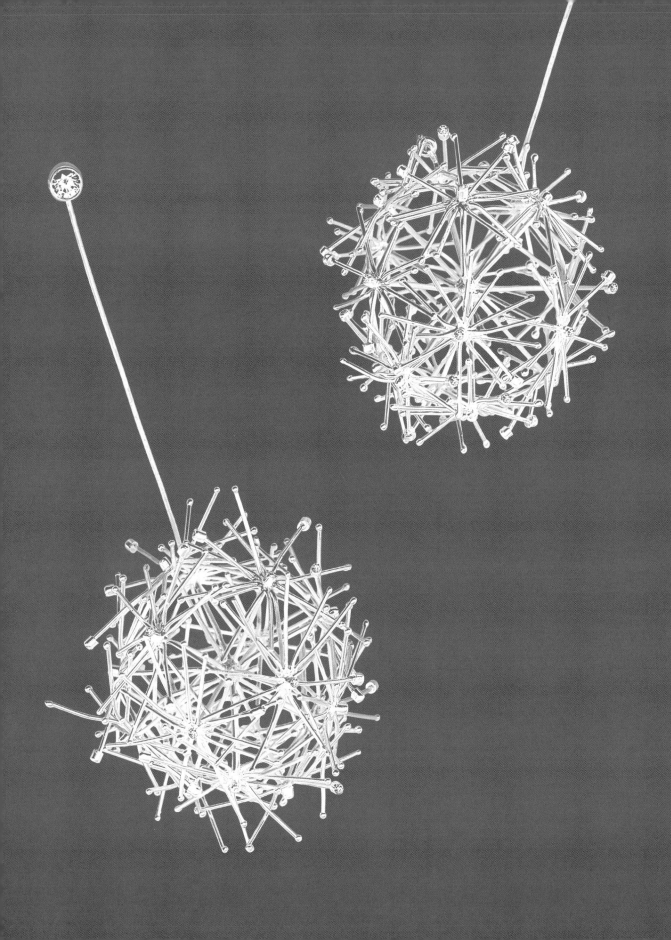

THE
VIRTUOSOS

Intriguing and beguiling expertise on display.
Testaments to opulent artistry that offer the pinnacle of luxury.

RIGHT Sketch for a platinum and diamond 'Coral' necklace, evoking an antique botanical print.

BELOW 'R-1829 Fine Rustic Diamond Leafside' ring of 22kt gold and diamonds.

CATHY WATERMAN

Platinum and diamonds entwine to form intricate foliage; delicate coloured gems make ethereal appearances on prongs and bezels. Cathy Waterman's exquisite, lace-like jewelry mesmerizes and inspires. Combining the robustness of precious metals with the magnificence of gemstones, she breathes diaphanous beauty into each of her pieces – the essence, if not the reality, of fragility. Time-honoured skills and techniques are married with a contemporary aesthetic to give jewelry that a modern-day Lady Guinevere would covet. 'I'm passionate about making beauty,' Cathy says. 'I have three children whose beauty I seek to approach in

my work. It's a worthy challenge, and making a jewel more beautiful than the last is what drives me.' Hollywood-born, Cathy studied Byzantine and Early Church history at college, which no doubt explains the graceful references to ancient and medieval history in her work. After law school and a brief film career, she decided to create jewelry, 'when I just couldn't find the exact pieces I wanted'. She began to draw them and opened a treasure trove that surprised and delighted her. Although often she sees fully finished jewels in her mind, she spends lots of time sketching. The composition is then fashioned by hand or carved into wax to be cast in either recycled 22kt gold or platinum. After twenty years' crafting exquisite works of art, her designs have recently become 'bolder and more driven by colour'. She travels the world, often with her family, in search of perfect jewels. They resonate with a special sense of occasion and capture wholeheartedly the mother–child bond that motivates their creator. Somehow this is jewelry that symbolizes a sublime rite of passage.

http://cathywaterman.com

RIGHT 'C-622 Fossilized Coral Kimono' pendant of 22kt gold and diamonds.

BELOW 'Br-747 Dancing Flowers' cuff of platinum and diamonds.

BELOW LEFT 'Fine Rustic Diamond Narnia' ring of platinum and diamonds.

BELOW 'Bow and Arrow' earrings of platinum, diamonds and cultured pearls.

RIGHT 'C-735 Ancient Carved' cameo in
Sleeping Beauty setting: diamonds, rubies,
orange sapphires and ruby chain.

BELOW 'Br-800 Trail of Tears' cuff of
fire opals, diamonds, rubies and sapphires.

BOTTOM 'Birthday' bracelet of rubies,
platinum and diamonds.

TOP 'Feather Prong' earrings of 22kt gold, London blue topaz and diamonds.

CENTRE 'Feather' earrings of platinum and diamonds.

RIGHT '11 Berry' pin of platinum, diamonds and yellow sapphires.

RIGHT 'Electric Bulb' necklace of 18kt yellow and white gold, with rose-cut diamonds (detachable bulb can be swapped with a pearl), *Tesserae* collection.

BELOW 'Aggressive' necklace of 18kt white gold, 22kt yellow gold and diamonds, *Lines* collection.

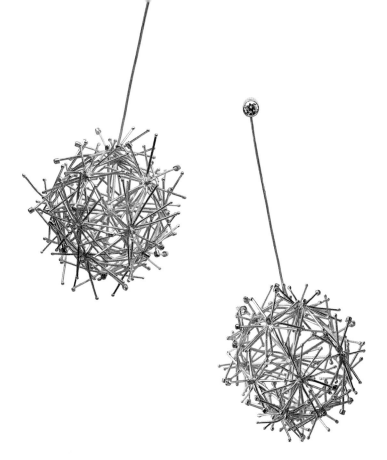

FANOURAKIS

Allow an exquisite symphony of gold and rose-cut diamonds to ignite your amorous thoughts. The maestro conductor is Athens-based Lina Diamandopoulo-Fanouraki, who suggests that 'there is no distinction between a jewelry designer and an architect or a choreographer'. Her melodic creations bear the hallmarks of classic elegance, yet they also display a tasteful eccentricity, thanks to technical panache and witty inventions. A seemingly mundane subject, delicate pencil shavings, is transformed into a magnificent golden brooch – an impossibly faithful replica. In similar vein, the classic diamond pendant necklace is revisited by an electrician: the

pendant becomes a 'lightbulb' hanging from a gold chain, mimicking to perfection a frail and twisted cable. 'I always experience a creative febrility by thinking I won't be able to create a new piece that's worth making. Then the actual idea comes and it's as if no one can stop me from then on,' Lina explains. 'It's at the workshop that the feast begins, trying to flesh my fantasies out into gold.' Each Fanourakis collection debunks the myth that elegance is an austere business: it is achieved with both gusto and simplicity, combining spontaneity with geometry, fantasy with practicality, and humour with tradition. Lina has been designing for some three decades and is aware that versatility is a big bonus when it comes to precious jewelry. Her *Tesserae* collection is the perfect example: it orchestrates rose-cut diamonds in timeless, heirloom designs that can be worn at any time of day. 'I would love to design jewelry for a modern ballet,' she says. 'A real jewelry piece for me is the one that makes you dream, the one that conveys joie de vivre.' Fanourakis creations are beyond 'real' in this respect.

www.fanourakis.gr

'Peoni' brooch of 24kt/22kt/18kt red and 18kt pink gold.

'Fortuni' bracelet of 22kt yellow and 18kt white gold, with rose-cut diamonds, *Folds* collection.

'Scales' bracelet of 22kt yellow and 18kt white gold, with diamonds.

'Moiré' bracelet of 22kt yellow gold, 18kt white gold and diamonds, *Gros Grain Ribbons* collection.

OPPOSITE, CLOCKWISE FROM TOP RIGHT

'Precious Coexistence' necklace of 18kt white and yellow gold, rose-cut diamonds and South Sea pearls, *Tesserae* collection.

'Griffes' earrings of 18kt white and pink gold, and rose-cut diamonds, *Tesserae* collection.

'Pencil Sharpener' brooch of 22kt yellow gold, 18kt white gold, diamonds and pigments.

'Butterfly' brooch of 22kt yellow gold, 18kt white gold and rose-cut diamonds, *Tesserae* collection.

GONZAGUE ZURSTRASSEN

Step into the royal court of a sumptuous wonderland: rare gemstones (fine rhodonites, vivid tourmalines, diamonds, spinels and Fanta-coloured spessartites) abound in a wide range of seductive shades, forming a dazzling array of bold yet feminine designs. Based in Thailand, Belgian designer Gonzague Zurstrassen is the master behind these one-of-a-kind, handmade creations. 'I've always been fascinated by noble materials and gemstones,' he recalls. 'I started collecting minerals when I was just eight. Each gem has its own personality. I love to draw out their unique eccentricities and character by positioning them against different stones

and materials.' Gonzague's creative drive stems from his family: his father is an art dealer, his brother an architect, and his uncle a celebrated painter. After graduating from the HRD Institute of Gemology in Antwerp as a certified gemologist, he started his career as an independent diamond broker. He then joined the renowned Mouawad family of jewelers, working closely with the eldest son, Fred, who later entrusted the company's Asian operation to him. Gonzague eventually set up his own business in Bangkok, 'but, to this day, Fred is still my mentor and inspiration,' he confides. Gonzague has complete control over the creative process in his studio, but still enjoys working as part of a team. One of his most enriching experiences was working alongside his brother, Matthieu, on his flagship gallery at the luxurious Soneva Kiri resort in Thailand. The project dovetailed perfectly with Gonzague's vibrant, artistic approach. His mind is always brimming with ideas, which can take anything from a few days to several months to develop. He then works closely with artisans to create the wax cast and complete the final design. His tantalizing talismanic pieces are made with exquisite craftsmanship and exude passion, romance and vivacity. Succumb to the temptation!

www.gzurstrassen.be

RIGHT 'Large Yellow Gold and Silver' necklace of 950cts of phrenites, rose quartz and chalcedony.

BELOW Top and side view of 'Pink Gold and Silver' ring of large 22ct natural brown zircon surrounded by 0.72cts of red spinels and 0.04cts of white diamonds.

BELOW RIGHT 'Large Yellow Gold' earrings of fine 34ct phrenites and rose quartz, with 5.5ct rose and green tourmalines.

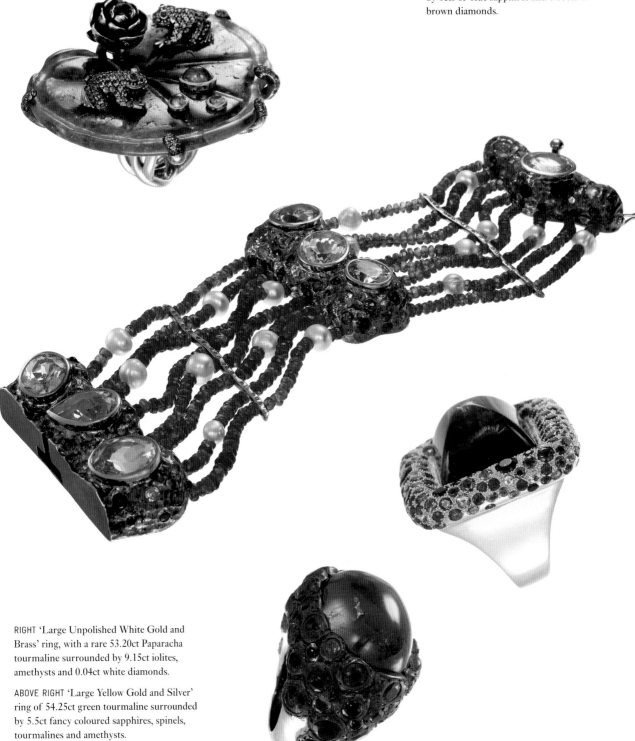

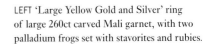

LEFT 'Large Yellow Gold and Silver' ring of large 260ct carved Mali garnet, with two palladium frogs set with stavorites and rubies.

BELOW 'Large Yellow Gold and Silver' bracelet of 150cts of flashy neon apatite, with 26.25cts of blue topaz and pearls, surrounded by 6cts of blue sapphires and 0.08cts of brown diamonds.

RIGHT 'Large Unpolished White Gold and Brass' ring, with a rare 53.20ct Paparacha tourmaline surrounded by 9.15ct iolites, amethysts and 0.04ct white diamonds.

ABOVE RIGHT 'Large Yellow Gold and Silver' ring of 54.25ct green tourmaline surrounded by 5.5ct fancy coloured sapphires, spinels, tourmalines and amethysts.

CLOCKWISE FROM RIGHT

'Yellow Gold' earrings of 37ct hot pink tourmalines, 6.2ct watermelon tourmaline slices, 0.70ct rough diamond slices and 0.68cts of polished diamonds.

'Large Yellow Gold and Silver' ring of 18.22cts of hot pink tourmalines surrounded by 22.06cts of amethysts and 0.05ct white diamonds.

'Yellow Gold and Silver' ring of rare 11ct rhodonite surrounded by 7.5cts of fancy coloured sapphires, garnets, amethysts and spinels.

'Large Yellow Gold and Silver' ring of 93.25ct pink quartz, surrounded by 3.8cts of pink and white sapphires and spinels.

CLOCKWISE FROM RIGHT

Necklace of South Sea pearls, resin, enamel and diamonds.

'Star Burst' earrings of jade, peridots and diamonds.

'Wind Chime' earrings of Colombian carved emeralds, pearls and diamonds.

RIGHT '3-D' earrings of chalcedonies, rubies, enamel and diamonds.

FAR RIGHT 'Claw' necklace of chalcedonies, rubies and diamonds.

HANUT SINGH

Prepare to fall for the astounding delicacy and sumptuous aura of Hanut Singh's jewelry, derived from a combination of old-world refinement and modern-day savvy. Hanut is an Indian prince whose grandmother, Princess Karam of Kapurthala, was an international sensation in the 1920s and '30s, bejewelled by the likes of Cartier and Van Cleef & Arpels. Little surprise that Hanut's work should seek to recall this noble family heritage. Each piece is a skilful and relevant nod to the above-mentioned era, making Hanut's work a modern rendition of the kind of ancestral jewelry commissioned under the Maharajahs' rule. The globetrotting designer – whose list of devoted clients reads like a *Who's Who* of the slickest tastemakers on Earth – describes his creative style as 'a well-made cocktail, a mix and a melody, with lashings from the past, present and future'. Finding the stones is what sparks Hanut's design journey. He has a predilection for antique rock crystals, Golconda diamonds and morganites. These form the main focus of his work, around which he creates the larger 3D piece. 'About eight years ago, I started with very simple shapes. But as time went on, and as I have studied the craft, I began doing slightly more elaborate pieces. I love the architecture of jewelry – so it's never too fussy but yet it's informed,' he explains. The flawless interplay of exquisite colours and rare stones, the Art Deco meets Indian fantasy theme, the intricate structure of each composition – all convey elegance and formal splendour. 'Jewelry is absolutely art!' Hanut exclaims. 'It requires the skill of a painter and the technique of an architect.' And quite possibly the grace and flair of a prince.

http://hanutsingh.com

LEFT Family heirloom: an ivory vanity set made by Asprey, London, for Hanut Singh's great-grandmother, flanked by photographs of his paternal and maternal grandmothers.

CLOCKWISE FROM RIGHT

'Principessa' earrings of morganites, moonstones and green amethysts.

Ring with Herkimer diamond and rubies.

'Claw' pendant of filigree gold, pearl, ruby and diamond.

'Graphic Flowers' earrings of tourmalines, fluorites and rubies backed in gold.

'Deco Framed' earrings with blue topaz and diamonds.

Earrings with turquoise Ganesha, gold, rubies and diamonds.

JESSICA MCCORMACK

Working in the jewelry department of Sotheby's, the famous auction house in London, Jessica McCormack was privy to some of the most extraordinary and rare jewels in the world. 'It made me want to create pieces that would be around long after I'm gone,' the New Zealander confides. 'I intend to create timeless pieces that can become heirlooms.' In her by-appointment-only salon/cabinet of curiosities in East London, her precious creations appear as small-scale works of art. 'I love the idea of jewelry existing both for the owner and the observer, so that it looks as stunning on the back as on the front. I also adore the concept of "secret diamonds" that are hidden from view, so that they are exclusively for the wearer,' she says. Jessica has an ingenious, emotionally charged versatility that translates her private clients' dreams into reality: 'I was commissioned to create a piece centred round a 20.27ct fancy yellow diamond called "Heaven's Hailstone,"' she recalls. 'It's an intelligent, mutating jewel that changes from a ring to a necklace to a clasp for a silk scarf. Each changing element of the jewel represents the client's three children.' Jessica's visionary spin is focused on reinvigorating the role of diamonds via cutting-edge designs that diffuse the traditional antique vibe and emphasize that diamond jewelry doesn't have to be brought out only for special occasions. 'When clients see me wearing the jewelry, they see that it can work with anything from jeans to black tie,' she says. Her *XIV* collection – inspired by the seven sins and seven virtues – is possibly the best example of the above, conveying Jessica McCormack's mercurial trademark. One should feel absolutely no guilt in lusting after these sublime offerings.

www.jessicamccormack.com

KATEY BRUNINI

Jewelry that could belong to a secret society of goddesses; jewelry whose muse is nature, with all its paradoxes of benevolence and volatility; jewelry on which the creativity of a citizen of the world has left its unmistakable imprint. Katey Brunini's work is a refined interpretation of modern luxury, 'exotic, erotic and alive'. California-based Katey (recipient of the Women's Jewelry Association's Fine Jewelry Designer of the Year, 2011) has spent her life studying the symbolism and poetry that now define her work. Each of her pieces reveals layers of intricate detail: goldsmithing techniques battle the luminescence of rare gemstones; sculptural silhouettes challenge an apparent fragility that turns out to be pure delicacy. 'One has to read between the lines in many pieces,' she notes. 'I'm passionate about the alchemical process of shape-shifting. Liquid/solid/gas come together in a dance, which creates a formulation of physical beauty to be carried on the body.' Katey's signature collections – *Twig*, *Vertebrae*, *DNA*, *Skipping Stones*, *Spider Web*, *Objects Organique*, *Spirit Animals* and *Body Armor* – reconcile science and myth as two interlaced forces. They are imbued with spirituality; almost shamanistic in their embrace of flora and fauna, mythology and sexuality, all the while giving pride of place to technical innovation. Katey acknowledges the complexities involved in each creation: 'It is a birth. I struggle, I contemplate and I nest on each idea. But when I decide on the physical form, the execution is swift compared to the incubation – almost surgical,' she explains. Hers is an ambitious enterprise but, as she points out, her timeless pieces 'have the ability to elevate the wearer's spirits'. What more can you ask?

www.kbrunini.com

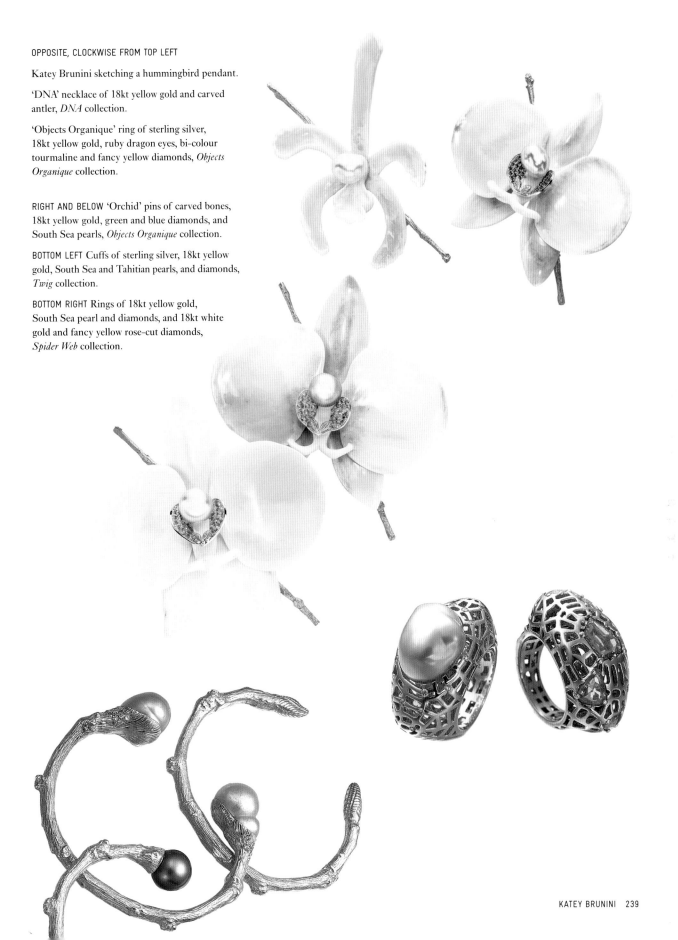

OPPOSITE, CLOCKWISE FROM TOP LEFT

Katey Brunini sketching a hummingbird pendant.

'DNA' necklace of 18kt yellow gold and carved antler, *DNA* collection.

'Objects Organique' ring of sterling silver, 18kt yellow gold, ruby dragon eyes, bi-colour tourmaline and fancy yellow diamonds, *Objects Organique* collection.

RIGHT AND BELOW 'Orchid' pins of carved bones, 18kt yellow gold, green and blue diamonds, and South Sea pearls, *Objects Organique* collection.

BOTTOM LEFT Cuffs of sterling silver, 18kt yellow gold, South Sea and Tahitian pearls, and diamonds, *Twig* collection.

BOTTOM RIGHT Rings of 18kt yellow gold, South Sea pearl and diamonds, and 18kt white gold and fancy yellow rose-cut diamonds, *Spider Web* collection.

RIGHT Necklace of 14kt pink gold chain, red spinel, 18kt pink gold cage, 333 pieces of diamond brilliants, *Chrysina aurigans* scarab from Costa Rica, *Scarabées de Beauté* collection.

BELOW Lito Karakostanoglou checking that her preserved scarab fits its gold casing perfectly before she glues the two together.

LITO KARAKOSTANOGLOU

Merging the old and the new, a seductive dash of antique flair with a touch of Art Nouveau, all blended with contemporary influences from around the world, Greek designer Lito Karakostanoglou offers a rare combination of luxurious, times-gone-by craftsmanship alongside a refreshing take on jewelry not simply as pieces of decoration but as everyday objects of desire. 'Often the process begins from sourcing an interesting material, which then dictates how the piece will evolve,' she says. 'Depending on the seasons, or my mood, this can develop in the most unexpected ways.' Perhaps the most striking examples are the preserved scarabs Lito found

in Madagascar, which she used when commissioned by the Galerie BSL to create a one-off collection, *Scarabées de Beauté*. Overcoming technical challenges, she used manual and laser techniques to preserve the scarabs' fragile colours and shapes, then magnified their beauty by encasing them in delicate golden cages and adorning them with small diamonds – an entomologist's extravagant dream. 'I've been designing for more than ten years,' Lito notes. 'My designs initially reflected spontaneity and freedom, which I got from discovering and experimenting with various materials – my favourite still being gold. Over the years, my jewelry has followed my own evolution. More elegant, more refined, more sexy!' Case in point her *Peacock* collection, with its colourful, enamelled, feather-like charms. 'For me, fine jewelry is closer to couture than to art,' she says. 'I design for women who dare to be themselves, women who have a style of their own, women who are fashionable in their unique way.' Lito is an innovator, fusing her true love for jewelry making with her dedication to the finest materials, ultimately bringing to fruition a vision for the unique, the flamboyant and the precious.

www.lito-jewelry.com

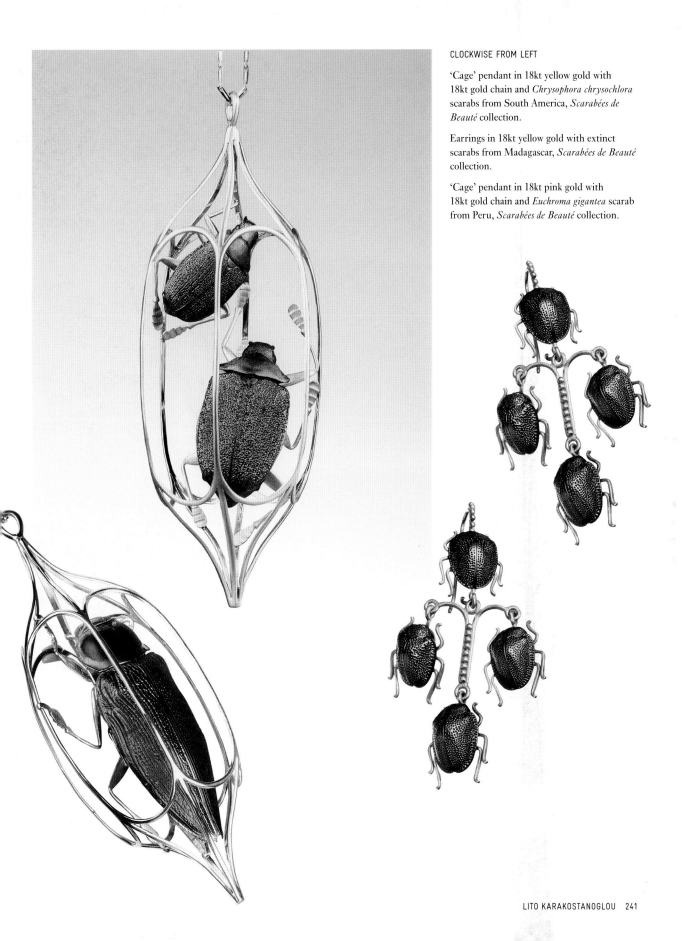

CLOCKWISE FROM LEFT

'Cage' pendant in 18kt yellow gold with 18kt gold chain and *Chrysophora chrysochlora* scarabs from South America, *Scarabées de Beauté* collection.

Earrings in 18kt yellow gold with extinct scarabs from Madagascar, *Scarabées de Beauté* collection.

'Cage' pendant in 18kt pink gold with 18kt gold chain and *Euchroma gigantea* scarab from Peru, *Scarabées de Beauté* collection.

RIGHT '3 Ring Mix': ring of 18kt pink gold with South Sea pearl, *Hive* collection; ring of 18kt pink gold and octagon-cut green amethyst, *Candy Girl* collection; ring of 18kt pink gold, Mediterranean coral starfish and brown diamonds, *Treasure Box* collection.

FAR RIGHT '3 Ring Mix': ring of 18kt pink gold with princess-cut pink tourmaline, *Candy Girl* collection; ring of 18kt pink gold and baguette-cut aquamarine, *Candy Girl* collection; ring of 18kt pink gold and Mediterranean coral starfish, *Treasure Box* collection.

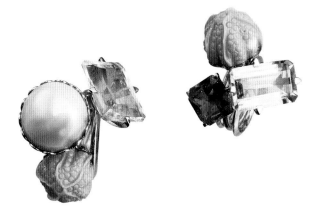

CENTRE 'Peacock' necklace of 14kt yellow gold, silver oxidized chain, rubies, pyrites, silver, 10kt pink gold enamelled Art Deco peacock pendant, *Peacock* collection.

ABOVE AND RIGHT 'Peacock' earring and pendant of 9kt pink gold and enamel, *Peacock* collection.

BELOW Bracelets of 14kt hammered pink gold and malachite studs/white marble studs, and ring of 18kt pink gold and oval malachite carved pebble, *Treasure Box* collection.

RIGHT '2 Ring Mix': ring of 18kt pink gold and baguette-cut labradorite in cone-net, *Hive* collection; ring of 18kt pink gold and coral rose, *I Do* collection.

CENTRE RIGHT '2 Ring Mix': ring of 18kt pink gold, trillion concave-cut Heliodor beryl and diamonds, *Candy Girl* collection; ring of 18kt gold and coral rose, *I Do* collection.

FAR RIGHT '2 Ring Mix': ring of 18kt pink gold and baguette-cut aquamarine in cone-net, *Hive* collection; ring of 18kt pink gold, coral rose and diamonds, *I Do* collection.

LUCIFER VIR HONESTUS

Precious metals seem to behave organically, as if morphed into a permanent melting state, evoking tormented branches that creep around classically faceted gems. This contrast enhances the exquisite beauty of the stone, as it sits in regal splendour in a fluid gold nest. Yin and yang, masculine and feminine, all at once. Apparently named after the first jeweler of medieval times, Lucifer Vir Honestus was founded in Milan by Luna Scamuzzi (principal designer) and Paolo Mandelli. 'Fourteen years ago Paolo introduced me casually to the method of casting wax. Bear in mind, I come from a family of architects, and was therefore convinced I'd be an architect as well – until I discovered, almost by chance, that I could create jewelry,' Luna explains. Completely self-taught, she was able to translate her architectural background into creating one-of-a-kind asymmetrical and sculptural pieces, each one the luxurious receptacle for magnificent stones. 'I source gems from all over the world. For each one, I create a new piece', she says. 'I work my wax as if to dress the stone and showcase it at its best.' A goldsmith and a setter work alongside Luna and Paolo in their Milan workshop, so the design duo are able to follow the birth of each piece from beginning to end, and can brainstorm and problem-solve on the spot. 'I don't "design" a jewel; I sculpt the model directly in wax. It's like writing or painting. Although I've now acquired more experience, you can still identify the same hand behind each work,' Luna notes. All indications suggest – and the magical allusions behind the brand name are a good marker – that Luna and Paolo could well be calligraphers of modern fairy tales.

www.lucifer-vir-honestus.com

LEFT Luna Scamuzzi modelling wax around her chosen stone in order to sculpt a ring.

RIGHT Necklace of 18kt rose gold, and white and grey baroque pearls.

BELOW Earrings of 18kt rose gold, emeralds, Ethiopian opals and diamonds.

ABOVE 'Granny's' ring of 18kt rose gold, emerald and diamonds.

RIGHT 'Solitaire' ring of 18kt rose gold and 5ct brilliant-cut diamond.

BELOW One-off pendant necklace in 18kt yellow gold, with brilliant-cut diamonds, natural star-cut aquamarine from Brazil, starfish in natural coral and Australian pearl, *Octopus* collection.

BOTTOM 'The Depths of Taormina' one-off pendant in 18kt yellow and white gold, with natural custom-cut aquamarine from Brazil and brilliant-cut diamonds, *Jewels of the Sea* collection.

RIGHT One-off earrings in 18kt yellow and white gold, with brilliant-cut diamonds and amber from Santo Domingo, *Jewels of the Sea* collection.

ABOVE One-off ring in 18kt yellow gold, with natural crude aquamarine from Brazil and brilliant-cut diamonds, *Jewels of the Sea* collection.

MASSIMO IZZO

Here is the myth: in a typically grand gesture, the gods once placed a single diamond in the middle of the ocean, which then transformed into the beautiful island of Sicily. Could it be that the workshop of Sicilian goldsmith Massimo Izzo, in historical Syracuse, is a direct emanation of these exceptional beginnings? His gargantuan creations certainly confirm that he is the standard-bearer for contemporary baroque jewelry: his flamboyant pieces could well be paraded through the streets in a modern-day Saturnalia. 'I started studying jewelry at the state institute of art in Syracuse at the age of 14, and I haven't stopped creating jewelry since,'

he says. 'I've always been attracted by the beauty of nature and all forms of art. I was at a crossroads – either becoming a restaurant chef or a goldsmith. I think I chose well, and I'm so glad I've invented my own style.' His uniquely sculpted, astonishingly opulent work has received considerable attention from the cognoscenti: devotees include the Swedish royal family, not to mention a swarm of international celebrities and premier-league clients, such as the Ritz Hotel and the Elsa Vanier Gallery in Paris, and the FD Art Gallery in New York. Massimo's *Jewels of the Sea* collection is emblematic of his extravagant interpretation of oceanic flora and fauna. Seahorses, starfish, crabs and octopuses act as theatrical receptacles for spectacular gems in a re-creation of underwater treasures. Gold in myriad shades is set with huge, often uncut gemstones, Sardinian coral, aquamarines, jade, turquoise, pearls and diamonds. The result? An abundance of luxurious, organic forms that emulate the chaos and exuberance of nature.

www.massimoizzo.com

MOLAYEM

Haute joaillerie unquestionably has its best days ahead, thanks to a cavalry of young enthusiasts who pay tribute to traditional techniques with novel, show-stopping marvels. Enter the Rome-based duo Diana and Stella Molayem, whose fabulous creations will inspire a few evening dresses to be taken out of storage. The sisters' cross-cultural family background (Persian antiquarians with Russian roots) explains why Molayem's style is not overtly Italian: 'Our jewelry reflects our open-mindedness. In a pair of earrings there could be traces of nineteenth-century Japanese art together with French Art Deco, or French Art Nouveau together with Oceanic art,' they say. This cross-pollination between different cultures and art movements forms part of their conviction that 'beauty generates beauty'. A predilection for diamonds and gems mounted simply is evidence of their classic eye and, in particular, of Stella's practical and minimalist character; the exuberant juxtaposition of rare stones and chimerical forms is more a reference to Diana's elaborate, baroque leanings. 'The part of the design process I enjoy most is drawing the object,' says Diana. 'When I create a pair of earrings, a necklace or a bracelet, I just let my creativity flow, and whatever comes into my mind is immediately drawn. I tend to draw the most strange and absurd pieces, whose parts are then mixed and matched to result in a superb hybrid. It's like finding the last element of an addictive puzzle.' The sisters' ambition is to expand the brand worldwide, but to keep it low-key and exclusive. Ultimately, they identify the Molayem label with the person-in-the-know whose 'jewels would be easily recognized, but not signed' – in itself, a sure sign of indulgent perfection.

www.molayem.it

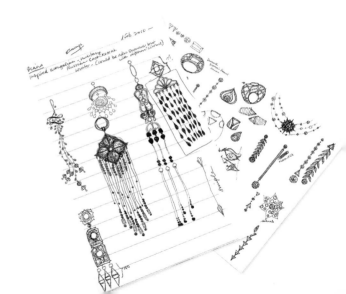

FAR LEFT 'Snake' earrings of emeralds and micro-mosaic of pearls, *Animalier* collection.

LEFT 'Pettorale Gem' chestplate of jade, turquoise, and precious and semi-precious stones, made for the 'Diaghilev PS' festival exhibition in St Petersburg, 2009.

ABOVE 'Floral' earrings of coral roses, cabochons, enamel and micro-mosaic of pearl leaves, *Coral* collection.

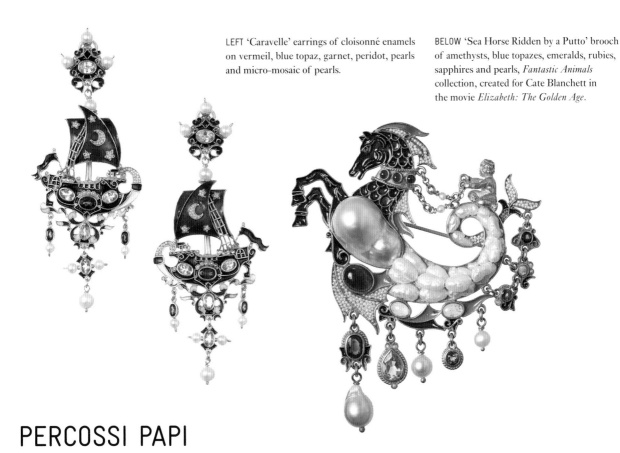

LEFT 'Caravelle' earrings of cloisonné enamels on vermeil, blue topaz, garnet, peridot, pearls and micro-mosaic of pearls.

BELOW 'Sea Horse Ridden by a Putto' brooch of amethysts, blue topazes, emeralds, rubies, sapphires and pearls, *Fantastic Animals* collection, created for Cate Blanchett in the movie *Elizabeth: The Golden Age*.

PERCOSSI PAPI

Time travel doesn't really exist … unless you're wearing a Percossi Papi creation, that is. Each intricate, highly crafted piece is an allegorical portrayal of a mythical or historical theme, so meticulously and superbly detailed that the wearer or observer is instantly transported to noble lands and legendary times. No detail is too small for collections that qualify as heritage in the making. 'I'm not a jewelry designer. I consider myself an *artifex*, an artist-artisan of ancient times,' Diego Percossi Papi declares. 'I'm self-taught; I studied architecture at university. With no technical basis at all, I initially tried the easiest way to represent reality: like prehistoric man inside his cave, I used the basic technique of profiling. Later I developed the more complex and precise technique of cloisonné, one of the first basic jewelry techniques, more ancient than lost wax.' Passionate about Mediterranean culture, Diego's creative inspiration is drawn from history: 'Greek tragedy, the Renaissance, the Egyptians, the Assyrians and the Romans,' he enthuses. 'And I absolutely love Baroque as dialectic and passion, the ultimate expression of the Mediterranean civilization.' The Rome-based artisan strives to connect with the object he is working on, in what he calls 'an authentic approach, the *genius loci* – creating an object in the knowledge of its context. If there is not a common key to understanding, it will just be a foreign object,' he explains. It's impossible not to feel emotionally responsive to Diego's work. His symbolic artifacts are medieval illuminations guaranteed to transfix both jewelry and art lovers alike.

www.percossipapi.com

BELOW Stones waiting to be embedded in a setting for a specially commissioned bracelet.

SYLVIE CORBELIN

A mysterious and sensual world, in which mythical characters coexist with naturalistic treasures; a poetic and baroque rhapsody combining precious gems, irregular stones and fine metals with expert craftsmanship and a Baudelairean aura. How Sylvie Corbelin is able to translate reveries into bewitching limited-edition jewelry becomes clear as soon as one steps into her workshop. Nestled between a rose garden and lush ivy in the secret heart of the Paul Bert flea market in Paris, the studio is charged with an enchanting atmosphere. Sylvie, a state-certified gemologist and member of the French National Syndicate of Antique Dealers, has long been fascinated by the traditions and history of Old Europe. Through her antique dealing, she stumbled upon a stock of rare and precious materials left by some retired Parisian lapidaries. 'I became a jewelry designer following a fascination for anything beautiful,' she states, and adds, 'It occurred to me that a jewelry piece is the smallest object one can wear that also tells stories.' Each opulent artwork is signed by the artist and registered at the National Industrial Property Institute. 'My creations follow a poetic exploration, a daydream that directs how the materials will come together. The most joyful experience is when, from my precise drawings, the piece is brought to life by the workshop.' Sylvie's collections include *Initiée*, with signature gold serpent rings; *Jardin*, testimony to her love of the countryside; *Impérator*, based on imperial insignia; *Lilith*, her take on secretive and archaic worlds; *Musique*, dedicated to joyful effervescence; and *Croisière*, an invitation to marine, celestial and terrestrial worlds, in which time is suspended. Each jewel case is made to measure by the finest craftsmen; each jewel purse is hand-sewn on silk woven in Lyon. Exceptional antiques from a phantasmagorical future.

www.sylvie-corbelin.com

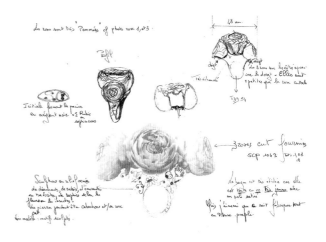

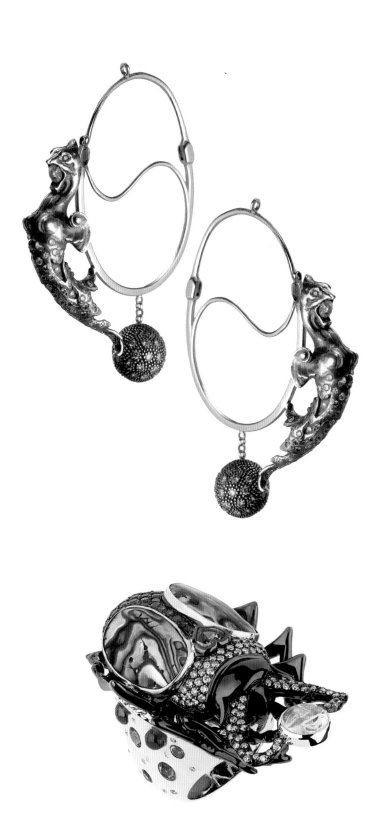

CLOCKWISE FROM TOP LEFT

'Chimères' hoop earrings in gold and silver, with white and black diamonds, *Lilith* collection.

'Black Magic' pendant with antique ebony carved head, gold and silver, pearls, diamonds, opal and rock crystal, *Musique* collection.

'Lucky Lucane' ring in gold and silver with diamonds, amethysts, moonstone and abalone mother of pearl, *Jardin* collection.

CLOCKWISE FROM RIGHT

'Pre Deep Nodo' double necklace of
hand-carved cameos from Sardonic shell,
with gold chain and silver cameo frames,
Psyche collection.

'F & M' earrings with hand-carved cameo
from Corneola shell and pearl, gold-plated,
Senses collection.

'Hand Me Over' bracelet with hand-carved
cameo from Corneola shell, brass chain and
gold-plated cameo frame, *Senses* collection.

'Agapi' cufflinks with hand-carved cameo
from Sardonic shell, *Psyche* collection.

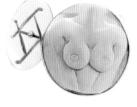

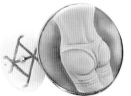

OPPOSITE ABOVE LEFT 'Widow's Blues'
necklace with hand-carved cameo from
Sardonic shell, pearl, brass chain and
gold-plated cameo frame, *Senses* collection.

OPPOSITE ABOVE RIGHT 'Awakening' necklace
with hand-carved cameo from Sardonic
shell, pearl, rose quartz, blue sapphire, garnet
stone, clear quartz, black obsidian, onyx and
hematite, *Senses* collection.

OPPOSITE BELOW Sketching a drawing on a
shell that has been cut to suit and attached to
a piece of wood for stability.

YATÜZ

What is the link between truck drivers and the ancient Italian craft of cameo carving? In short, the jewelry brand Yatüz. The name combines the founders' initials with the word *tüz*, meaning 'fire of the soul'. According to the Rome-based designers Yumiko Saito and Angela Dorazio, 'Truck drivers' soft-porn posters of posing seductive girls, although sexual, also address the fertile, powerful female body, inviting male fantasy but also invoking protection.' They add: 'What is a sexual fantasy, if not a desperate longing for comfort, security and unity? We believe jewelry is like the patterns on fur or a feather, or the colours or smell of a plant

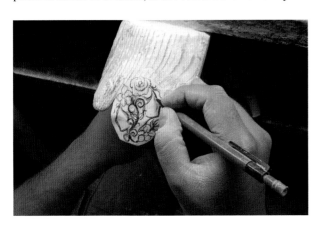

– a conveyor of subliminal messages.' Yumiko and Angela have resurrected the once highly revered Italian cameo tradition, but in so doing have added a lighthearted review of the zeitgeist, raunchy humour and a political agenda. Delving into ancient mythology and popular narratives concerning the role of women in society, they conclude, 'There was a peaceful world in ancient times, where female mystery was creatively worshipped, until destructive male gods began to take over.' With the help of skilled artisan carvers – who often add little details of their own, in an appreciative endorsement of the duo's intentions – the designers' drawings are translated into one-off jewels that adorn aristocratic pearl necklaces, made from the shells of the *Cassis madagascariensis* and *Cassis rufa* families, which give the distinctive pink, white and brown colouring. 'It's a very rare and one-of-a-kind art, as the real shell-carved cameo, such as ours, is only made in one village in Italy –Torre Del Greco,' they point out, 'nowhere else.' Yatüz's iconographic creations, literally, could not be more special.

www.yatuz.com

THE
AVANT-GARDISTS

When art becomes wearable … and you become the gallery.
Experimental compositions to suit the body
and the display cabinet.

RIGHT 'Dance 01' bodice of cow leather and cotton, *Crush* collection.

BELOW Fine steel cable – symbol of Hong Kong – is an unusual juxtaposition against soft tassels and pompoms.

OPPOSITE ABOVE LEFT 'Balance Out' necklace of hand-dyed silk pompoms, Indian hand-dyed silk tassels and fine steel cable, *City Roamers* collection.

OPPOSITE ABOVE RIGHT AND BELOW LEFT 'Bodice' necklace of hand-dyed silk pompoms, Indian hand-dyed silk tassels and fine steel cable, *City Roamers* collection.

OPPOSITE BELOW RIGHT 'One Eyeball' necklace of hand-dyed silk pompoms, Indian hand-dyed silk tassels and fine steel cable, *City Roamers* collection.

CCCHU

The study of movement and our disconnection with our surroundings are at the heart of CCCHU's design philosophy. The Hong Kong-based husband-and-wife team Ching Ching Wong and Michael Chu ignore fashion trends and concentrate instead on addressing jewelry's potential to promote wellbeing and vigour – hence their two energizing collections for pioneering urban tribes. The *Crush* collection features nude leather yokes interlaced with cotton strings, offering poetic yet archetypal outfits for hip ballerinas: 'Stripes, bells and fringes encourage sweat and jovial movements; the accessories were inspired by dance costumes and totems,' the pair explain. *City Roamers*, on the other hand, presents a series of colourful necklaces held together by a steel wire frame, almost like an airy corset, giving a futuristic yet joyful folkloric vibe, complete with hand-dyed silk tassels and pompoms. These, they say, are 'influenced by the horror paintings and comics of the Japanese manga artist Mizuki Shigeru. The neckpieces were created for guidance and protection while living in the city.' Experimentation with jewelry as a form of harnessing is an important feature of CCCHU's work, so much so that their pieces not only accompany the wearer's movements, but also magnify bodily expressions. 'We see jewelry as a form of cosmetics – you put a piece on your neck and it immediately changes how a person perceives your face,' they enthuse. 'We also wanted to create jewelry that elicits energy and motions from the wearer, and for that reason we bend, twist, squeeze and sew to test the characteristics and possible limitations of each chosen material over roughly a couple of weeks.' It is jewelry that is visionary in technique, style and execution. Dance and prance accessories just became a necessity.

www.ccchu.com

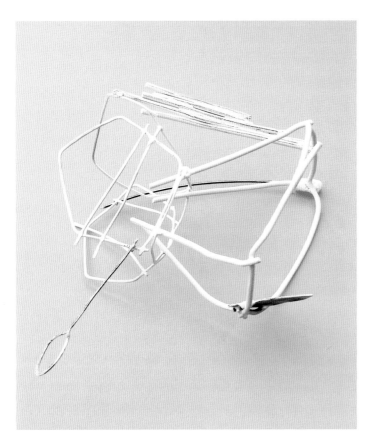

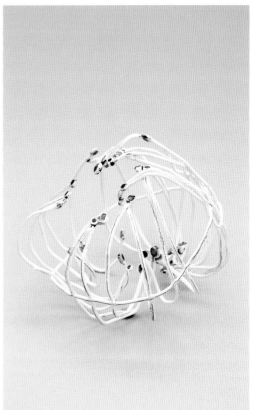

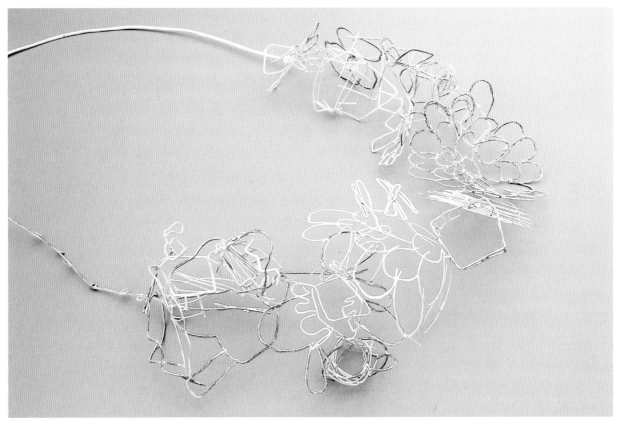

FARRAH AL-DUJAILI

Eerie and airy, bold yet somehow immaterial, enamel-coated copper wires intersect and entwine, morphing into playful hybrid forms. The course the metal takes is organic and unpredictable, much like wool that has been unwound and then rewound on an imaginary spool, or pencil marks that appear on paper when the imagination flows freely. The work of Farrah Al-Dujaili, who is based in Birmingham in the UK, evokes 3D drawing; an impulsive way of sketching in the air that produces beguiling fashion jewelry. 'Drawing plays a key role in my design methodology as a subconscious act. It reduces thoughts into symbols, marks, colours and patterns,' she explains. 'Fragments are created and later constructed to produce the idiosyncratic detailing that appears in my drawings. I work within an intuitive mix of drawing and making that crosses over and intertwines.' Light, blue-hued touches of pencil, crayon and watercolour heighten the structural presence, emphasizing the dialogue between drawing and making. Farrah concentrates initially on how a piece looks sculpturally before focusing on practicalities and how it will be worn. She summarizes her working procedure: 'The spontaneous making process requires quick aesthetic judgments – playing with angles and positioning forms – in an attempt to achieve a mixture of space and detail. It is in the construction of these fragments that the layering of line and form creates the detailing that appears in my design proposals. The unexpected detailing from an extra hammer mark or an additional length of wire is where the excitement of the making process comes together.' There is an undeniable sense of mystery in the work, as if each piece is formulating its own unique outcome. Farrah's magic lies in her ability to orchestrate preternatural happenings.

http://farrahal-dujaili.blogspot.com

RIGHT Though she works on several pieces simultaneously, Isabel Dammermann always takes time to reflect on every aspect of her finished articles.

BELOW LEFT 'Gigas I' ring of silver, brush, 18kt gold, silicon and azurite.

BELOW RIGHT 'Gigas II' ring of 18kt gold, shibuichi (copper/silver alloy) and barite.

OPPOSITE, CLOCKWISE FROM TOP LEFT

'Perpetua II' pendant of shibuichi, silver, ebony and cotton.

'Perpetua I' pendant of shibuichi, silver, ebony, 18kt gold and silver.

'Menhir' earrings of silver, Plexiglas and transparent paper.

'Limni' brooch of shibuichi, silver and found stone.

ISABEL DAMMERMANN

Isabel Dammermann is a curator of improbable encounters and accidental mergers. Her organic and mineral creations, imbued with a rich poetic vein, have a unique, otherworldly elegance – part raw simplicity, part fragmented sculpture. In her work, she oscillates 'between conscious choices and unconscious arrangements'. As she explains: 'I collect elemental materials and objects, shroud them with intuitive impressions, and see how they respond to each other, how they communicate. They meet in order to separate again, or come together in a new form.' The process is, she says, 'about reaching the perception of concealed possibilities that lie within the things that surround us'. Currently based in Hanover, Isabel believes she was influenced by her creative grandmother, who introduced her to art: 'She also used to do some goldsmithing. We did tinkering, pottery and painting together, and when I finished my A-levels I already knew that it would be much easier for me to do handwork – a fortuitous happenstance.' Isabel recently graduated from the Alchimia school of contemporary jewelry in Florence, and launched NOI ('us' in Italian) with a group of fellow ex-students. The creative collaboration involves 'nine girls from nine different countries with nine different styles, with the intention of organizing jewelry exhibitions – for example, in the Lalaounis museum in Athens and in Istanbul'. Isabel notes that, 'With every project I get to discover new things that lead to a deeper understanding of myself and my surroundings.' As she points out, 'One sees what one sees. However, one also experiences a tension between emotion and rationality. My work opens a fictional access to reality; it is a metaphorical view of the world.' And what a mesmerizing spectacle that is.

www.isabeldammermann.com

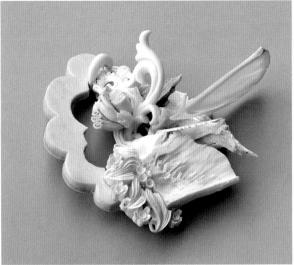

TOP LEFT 'Germinate' necklace of pre-ban ivory, steel, brass, mule deer antlers, cow and ox bones, nutria teeth, pigeon skull, plastic and diamonds, all found or repurposed, *Embodiment* series (private collection).

ABOVE LEFT 'Cluster' brooch of cow bone, deer bone and antler, nutria teeth, Turkish catfish spine, rabbit scapula, silver, plastic and diamond, *Embodiment* series (private collection).

TOP RIGHT 'Acanthus' neckpiece of antler, eighteenth-century frame fragments and gold leaf, *Wearable – Vestige 2011* series.

ABOVE RIGHT 'Chrysanthemum Morifolium' object of ribs, baculum and various bones, antler, seventeenth- and nineteenth-century frame fragments, and 23.5kt gold leaf, *Object – Vestige 2011* series (private collection).

RIGHT 'Swag' neckpiece of antler, bone, seventeenth- and nineteenth-century frame fragments, and gold leaf, *Wearable – Vestige 2011* series.

BOTTOM Small burs, files and odd bits of silver and gold share Jennifer Trask's workbench with tiny white snake vertebrae destined to become earrings.

JENNIFER TRASK

Jennifer Trask's unique take on jewelry involves highlighting reason and intuition but blurring the lines between art and adornment to produce creative, hybrid compositions. The raw elements in her box of treasures unite in an organic symphony of baroque perfection, offering, according to the designer, 'a romanticized vision of nature'. Found and repurposed materials that are a testament to Jennifer's fascination for biology – bones, antlers, teeth, pre-ban ivory, steel, brass, pigeon skulls – dodge a future of slow decay in an artistic rebirth, in which the invisible (diamonds are hidden from view) and the thought-provoking (what do we carry with us in our bones?) form the main *coup de théâtre*. 'I would say the most challenging aspect is function,' says Hudson-based Jennifer. 'Considering my use of unconventional materials and techniques, it's often difficult to make wearable pieces that function as easily, but invisibly, as traditional necklace clasps, for instance.' An example is to be found in the *Wearable – Vestige* series, in which feather-like branches and chrysanthemum overgrowths seem to have broken away from an artwork's frame to become the grafts for necklaces and brooches. Jennifer is an artist who works in various formats and who came to jewelry from an art background, first by making wearable work in graduate

school, simply because the format served her aims at the time. 'Now I don't make anything I wouldn't want to wear, keep or look at myself,' she says. 'I strive for the pieces to speak to universal concerns, to be pertinent yet accessible on multiple levels. If you respond to the work on a purely visual level: great! If you relate to my intent or have a sentimental response: terrific!' How could we not?

www.jennifertrask.com

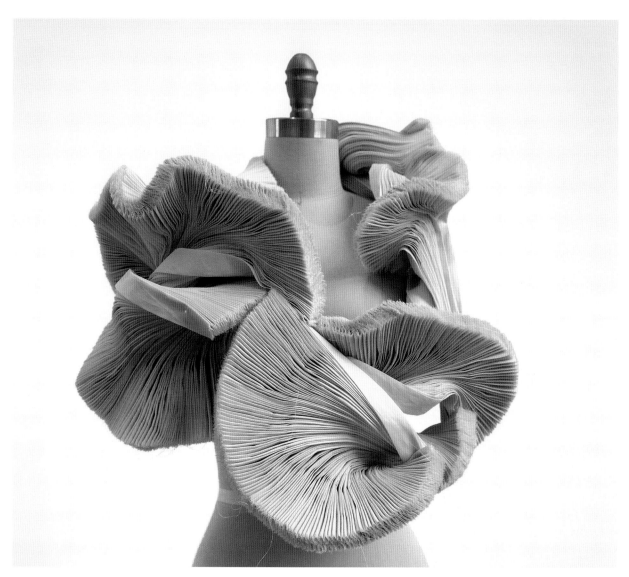

KWODRENT

Lengths of monochromatic textile seem to have been manipulated by an invisible miracle worker; a hint of chaos is offset by a rationality that provides a sense of objectivity and compositional logic. This is the work of kwodrent, a Singapore-based multidisciplinary design studio run by Grace Tan, whose ongoing *100 neckpieces* project is a study of a series of wearable objects based on simple mathematical equations and a particular type of construction. 'When I first started working on kwodrent, I was preoccupied with the relationship between clothes and the human body. The series rapidly grew from a handcrafted clothing line to include wearable fabric structures,' says Grace. 'I then became intrigued by the idea that something we wear on our bodies could be abstracted or transformed into other objects.' This is why she envisages jewelry as 'additional layers of clothing that should exist and function as autonomous micro-compositions'. The kwodrent series is a continuing body of work – hence a numbering system – and each new piece is a development of the earlier works. 'The concept of continuity and spontaneity is crucial in the progression of the series,' she shares. Graceful yet complex, the pieces are shaped by the distinctive methodology at work: 'I very rarely sketch the design. I work freely with my hands, allowing the material to guide me while I try to apply my techniques. I am constantly waiting for something to mutate or fall out of place to trigger something I have never seen or expected' – that extra, elusive dose of 'incompleteness' that allows us, the wearers, to interact with the work, and to immerse ourselves in Grace's intuitive/scientific endeavours.

www.kwodrent.com

BELOW RIGHT Crown in triple 24kt gold-plated
metal (one of three) worn by Cate Blanchett
in the Sydney Theatre Company production,
The War of the Roses, 2009.

BOTTOM In Lisa Cooper's studio, her paintings
make a stunning backdrop for her beguiling
creations, including 'Attention Task IV'
hand-gilded thorns.

OPPOSITE, CLOCKWISE FROM TOP LEFT

Veil in triple rhodium-plated metal.

'Wing for Icarus' in triple 24kt gold-plated
metal.

Untitled cuff in triple 24kt gold-plated metal.

Helmet in triple 24kt gold-plated brass.

Untitled cuff in triple rhodium-plated metal.

LISA COOPER

A finely crafted gold wing, a gilded helmet with gossamer-like foliage, flamboyant cuffs and a magnificent crown. The sacred apparel of a fallen angel, perhaps? Or Olympian costumes for a bacchanalia, or regalia to help induce Corpus Christi-like fervour? Australian artist Lisa Cooper is passionate about flora and precious metals … and the symbolic resonances created when the two are combined. 'I begin by identifying a body part that I want to create a piece for, then it's all about growing the assemblage and relying on instinct,' she says. 'Each piece develops in the same way that a painting or an arrangement of flowers does, by building up sections, elements and their relation to the whole.' With a Ph.D. in video art, Lisa's point of departure in all her projects is artistic. Although her work has a direct and intimate relationship to the body, her technique and objects of attention recall the Renaissance craftsmen who painstakingly soldered religious artifacts. 'My wearable work was born of, or has its lineage in, more elaborate sculpture,' she explains. 'The revelation that it could translate into adornment was organic and compelled by private collaborations.' She was commissioned to create three identical crowns for the Sydney Theatre Company's production of *The War of the Roses*, in which, for the first hour, Cate Blanchett 'wore my crown on an empty stage, while gold foil was falling from the heavens over the entire space. It was amazing.' Without question, Lisa writes poetry in three dimensions, alchemizing gold or rhodium into runes that have incantatory power and seraphic glory. A pursuit touched by grace.

www.doctorcooper.com.au

MICHELLE LOWE-HOLDER

Portraits of Rubenesque seventeenth-century royals wearing large lace collars and cuffs come to mind when we contemplate Michelle Lowe-Holder's dramatic pieces. It is as if these lavish aristocratic accessories have been isolated and redesigned in a contemporary way. Canadian-born and London-based Michelle has invented a new form of language through her highly crafted, wearable designs. By teaming up with the photographer Polly Penrose, she has also begun to explore how to free her pieces from the constraints of high fashion. 'We have been carefully casting models,' she says, 'and trying to create images that question the aesthetic of beauty.' Their unconventional sitters highlight fashion taboos – too young, too old, too full-figured, too athletic… 'To have the freedom to develop these images with my accessories, which use unrecognized materials and by way of hand labour become special and have value, on some level seems to fit the ideas we are trying to explore.' Michelle salvages handcrafted details – often vintage off-cuts, scraps from previous collections and ends of lines – and upcycles them through a committed and creative ethical policy of zero waste. 'It's a very organic process of making, looking and shaping. The process itself creates the pieces,' she muses. 'I was mentored by the London College of Sustainable Fashion for my first jewelry/accessory collection in 2010, and that's why I then decided to focus on sustainability. My idea was always to make the detail the piece, as opposed to applying the detail to clothing.' Each season is based on a particular handcraft speciality – ribbon art, flocking, crochet – which is revisited in a unique way. Michelle is spearheading nothing less than the responsible reinvention of craft heritage.

www.lowe-holder.com / http://lowe-holder.blogspot.com

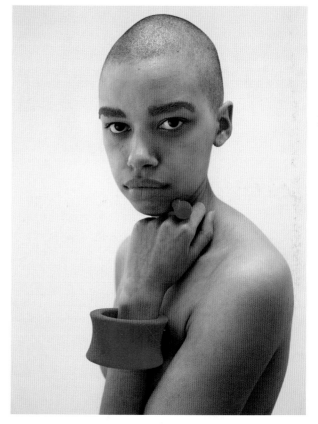

OPPOSITE TOP LEFT 'Flock and Fold' lantern cuffs in cotton and copper foil, *AW11* collection, modelled by Theresa Williams.

OPPOSITE TOP RIGHT 'Ribbon Reclaim' neck choker in cotton and crochet with flocked hardware, *AW10* collection, modelled by Bronwyn Lowe.

OPPOSITE BOTTOM LEFT 'Ribbon Reclaim' necklace in velvet and crochet, *AW10* collection, modelled by Sinead Feeney.

OPPOSITE BOTTOM RIGHT 'Flock and Fold' bangle and ring with flocked hardware, *AW11* collection, modelled by Theresa Williams.

ABOVE 'Flock and Fold' neckpiece with grey tartan mixed fibre textile, flocked beads and flocked hardware, *AW11* collection.

OPPOSITE 'Giant Charm Bracelet with Ceramic Charms' in earthenware and porcelain, with brass chain.

BELOW 'Floral Pomander' charm in hand-built porcelain.

RIGHT 'Doll Face' charm and 'Regency Pearl' necklace in slipcast earthenware.

BOTTOM Ceramicist's territory: Nicola Malkin's bright and sunny workshop.

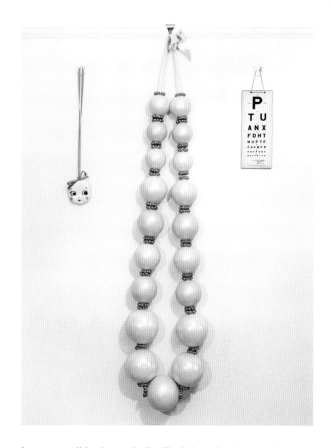

NICOLA MALKIN

This is how Alice must have felt after being shrunk in that charming yet daunting Wonderland. Nicola Malkin's apparently girly, ceramic sculptures are in fact monumental theatrical performances – jewelry expanded to an immense scale. 3D ceramic design has never been so intriguing. 'I use jewelry as a vehicle to tell a story. It's more than simply decorative and can be given to show love, appreciation or honour. I create jewelry because its structure is uniquely and immediately desirable,' Nicola explains. 'My giant charm bracelets are hung with grapefruit-sized trinkets that refer to everyday objects and are linked together in a way and an order that become strikingly symbolic. Each bracelet develops its own narrative, as new charms can be collected by the owner and hung at any time, bringing a deeper engagement and emotional relationship with the sculpture.' The sheer size of the creations, their tactile qualities and the playfulness of the elements and colours are utterly compelling. After graduating from Camberwell College of Arts in London, Nicola won a Crafts Council Development Award. Now based in Surrey, she is also an associate lecturer at Central St Martins in London. Her creative and production processes are intricately bound together, due to the unpredictable nature of her material. 'The casting part, which is the really hands-on part before the work goes near the kiln, is when things are a bit more challenging yet exciting for me,' she exclaims. A piece never fully develops the way she originally envisaged, but evolves as she starts to make 3D models (she generally makes several versions before deciding on the final product). Her next project? To create a charm bracelet from the shrunken heads of former boyfriends. Yes, Nicola's work is impressive ... and also full of therapeutic humour.

www.nicolamalkin.com

RIGHT 'Calcium Beauty' necklace made of plastic lids from German milk packs, *Calcium Beauty* series: Cherry Boonyapan design.

BOTTOM 'Copied No 1' necklace of porcelain and gold-plated brass, *Copied* series: Cherry Boonyapan design.

OPPOSITE, CLOCKWISE FROM TOP LEFT

'SuperNatural' bracelet in beech wood, *SuperNatural* collection: Lina Lundberg design.

'SuperNatural' necklace in beech wood, *SuperNatural* collection: Lina Lundberg design.

'Lilith' necklace of bicycle chain parts, silver and onyx, *Lady Lilith* collection: Lina Lundberg design.

'Rosie' rings of bicycle chain parts and silver, with onyx and with cultured pearls, *Lady Lilith* collection: Lina Lundberg design.

SPREEGLANZ

We live in an age in which public and private sponsorship of the arts is under threat. So when individuals step forward to support upcoming talent, it is important that their initiatives are recognized. Enter German product designers Heidi Fleiss and René Hofmann. This devoted duo have established a live/work collective studio in Berlin, with a fully funded one-year residency offered to gifted newcomers, whereby 'they can make their dreams come true with professional equipment and without any commercial constraints'. Under the Spreeglanz umbrella, innovative jewelry designers from all over Europe populate a bustling den of creativity that produces fabulously experimental, forward-looking work. Two young talents, in particular, have been spotted on the style-watch radar: Thai-born Cherry Boonyapan, based in Germany, and Lina Lundberg from Sweden. Cherry conveys a poetic touch, as in her *Calcium Beauty* series, in which pristine white mineral scales heighten a delicate, flower-like generosity. 'Lines, colours, sharpness, form, surface and contrasts inspire me. Friends would often call my work "arty", but in the end they find it hard to put in a box,' she says. Lina, meanwhile, has a playful approach, with bold pieces that emanate otherworldly glamour. 'The starting points in my work often arise from a fascination with a material. The challenge becomes to create a balance between the product, the user and the context,' she explains. 'I want to make the wearer feel rich, but not necessarily in monetary terms.' A sense of enigma – Unidentified Fashion Object – characterizes the work of both of these gifted young designers who have reinvigorated the world of fashion jewelry. Their 'new brigade' moniker is well deserved.

http://spreeglanz.com

CLOCKWISE FROM RIGHT

'Porcelain Collar', glazed, *Handle With Care* collection.

'Ringchain' of glazed and gilded porcelain, with 925 silver chain, *AU[79]* collection.

'Porcelain Chain 32 Links' necklace in biscuit, with 925 silver chain, *Handle With Care* collection.

Plastron of gilded porcelain, *AU[79]* collection.

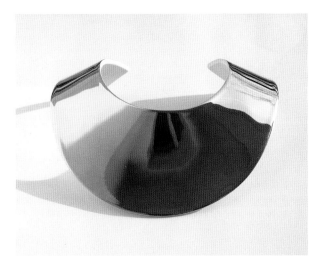

UNCOMMON MATTERS

Re-appropriating the noble qualities of porcelain in unexpected ways was at the heart of Amélie Riech's endeavour to launch handmade limited-edition 'couture' jewelry within 'uncommon matters', her artistic/design platform. Each piece – crafted using traditional techniques in the historic porcelain region of Thuringia in Germany – is an innovative celebration of femininity, in its purest form. Shapes are moulded directly from a woman's silhouette in order to embrace the wearer's body, while smooth lacquered surfaces in a simple palette of platinum, gold and pure white add a delicate sheen. These futuristic decorative shields suggest purity and fragility, and are so sensual that they could pass for diffusing tactile pheromones. 'I consider myself an artist, and stereotypical thinking and other restrictions are very dissatisfying and counter-productive for me,' Amélie states. 'I'm always curious and searching for playful and experimental ways of expressing new aspects of my universe.' She works studiously to gather inspiration, then to establish moods and build collages, slowly focusing on the body when it comes to defining proportions and shapes. 'I build lots of prototypes in wax or other material before starting with the actual mould-making,' she explains. 'I'm getting more and more interested in "contemporary couture", wearable art. Lately my work has evolved around glass and the combination of various substances; designs that stand for the reciprocity between craftsmanship and innovation in both technique and material.' In this respect, Amélie is not a typical jewelry designer: her design duties extend beyond 'mere' accessory making. But she has developed a passionate bond with jewelry, which she believes offers 'great latitude; it doesn't have to be functional in the first place'. Uncommon matters … or how to wear your art on your sleeve.

www.uncommonmatters.com

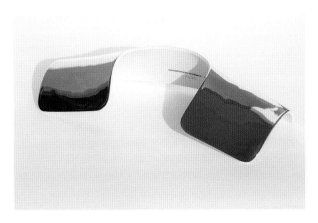

RIGHT Wood and leather cuffs designed for *Zero + Maria Cornejo* 2011 resort collection.

BELOW Victoria Simes's Bowery studio and showroom, resembling an art space suited for experimental performances.

OPPOSITE ABOVE 'One Side' chain necklace in silver and horsetail, with silver chain, *Victoria Simes* collection.

OPPOSITE BELOW 'Silver Tassel' necklace in yarn and silver tail, with chain, *Victoria Simes* collection.

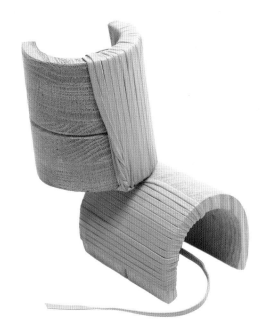

VICTORIA SIMES

This hotly sought-after stylist-cum-jewelry designer promotes natural materials as wearable art forms. In her *Saltalamacchia* collection (sentimentally named after her grandmother), downtown New York darling Victoria Simes sharpens up overtly androgynous, bewitchingly fetishistic, forcefully talismanic pieces that juggle urban grit and primal materials – an organic assortment of wood, leather, feather, horse and human hair, soon to be complemented by metals and unpolished diamonds. 'Sometimes it starts with a very abstract drawing that I sketch, but I always begin by prepping every single piece, from one end to the other,' Victoria explains. 'I make sure to design a solid, full collection – pieces that are wearable for everyday as well as pieces that are editorial high fashion. I also don't mind revisiting older designs and improving them as I fine-tune my techniques.' Her distinctly off-piste collection includes red oak cuffs with knotted leather overlays and long, sensual horsehair necklaces like thinned-out hybrid manes. The designs confront 'safe', middle-of-the-road jewelry through an innovative and edgy prism ('for people who have no fear', quips Victoria). Her approach is artistic in essence and embraces collaborations – the most defining of which have included work with maverick fashion designer Maria Cornejo for the Zero + Maria Cornejo line and with curator/mentor/friend Stephanie Pappas. 'I've also started to work on *the* dream project with my partner, architect Daniel Holguin. We're developing a collection called "Jewellery 4 Architecture". It's using the materials I work with, but changing the scale to something in between jewelry and architecture,' she enthuses. The new guard has a queen.

www.victoriasimes.com

RIGHT 'Tail' scarf in tail and yarn, *Victoria Simes* collection.

BELOW 'Tribal' necklace in knotted leather and tail, *Victoria Simes* collection.

BELOW RIGHT 'Curve Wood Leather' necklaces designed for *Zero + Maria Cornejo* 2011 resort collection.

ABOVE 'Knotted' bracelet in leather and tail, with silver endings, *Victoria Simes* collection.

CENTRE 'New Tassel' necklace in leather, tail, gunmetal chain and yarn, *Victoria Simes* collection.

RIGHT 'Angle Feather' necklace in sterling silver, leather and feathers, *Victoria Simes* collection.

RESOURCES

Some of the best purveyors of jewelry in the world: retail, galleries and online shops.

AUSTRALIA
Alice Euphemia, Melbourne:
www.aliceeuphemia.com
Eastern Market, Melbourne:
www.easternmarket.com.au
e.g.etal, Melbourne: http://egetal.com.au
Fallow, Brisbane: http://fallow.com.au
LEFT, Melbourne:
http://leftmelbourne.blogspot.com.au
Museum of Old and New Art, Hobart:
http://mona.net.au
Ondene, Sydney: www.ondene.com
Ricarda, Perth: www.ricarda.com.au
ZEKKA, Perth and Shenton Park:
http://zekka.com

AUSTRIA
Skrein Schmuckwerkstatt, Vienna:
www.skrein.at/schmuck

BAHRAIN
Yazi: www.yazibahrain.com

BELGIUM
RA13, Antwerp: http://shop.ra13.be

BRAZIL
Daslu, São Paulo: www.daslu.com.br
NK Store, São Paulo: www.nkstore.com.br
Surface to Air, São Paulo: www.surfacetoair.com

CANADA
Galerie Noel Guyomarc'h, Montreal:
www.galerienoelguyomarch.com
Holt Renfrew, Calgary, Edmonton, Montreal,
Ottawa, Quebec City, Toronto, Vancouver,
Vaughan, Winnipeg: www.holtrenfrew.com
Joseph-Anthony Fine Jewelry, Windsor, Ontario:
www.joseph-anthony.com
Rue Pigalle, Toronto: www.ruepigalle.ca
Serpentine, Toronto: http://theserpentine.net

DENMARK
Graff, Copenhagen: http://graff-cph.dk
Storm, Copenhagen: www.stormfashion.dk

DUBAI
Harvey Nichols: www.harveynichols.com
s*uce: www.shopatsauce.com

FINLAND
Lumi, Helsinki: http://lumiaccessories.com

FRANCE
107RIVOLI, Boutique des Arts Décoratifs, Paris:
www.lesartsdecoratifs.fr/english-439/
107rivoli-the-boutique

Atelier des Bijoux Créateurs (online shop):
www.atelier-bijoux-createurs.com
Barichella, Nice: www.barichella.fr
Caratime (online shop): http://fr.caratime.com
Centre Commercial, Paris:
http://centrecommercial.cc
Colette, Paris: www.colette.fr
Franck et Fils, Paris: www.francketfils.fr
Gago, 20 rue Fabrot, 13100 Aix-en-Provence
Galerie BSL, Paris: http://galeriebsl.com
Galerie Elsa Vanier, Paris: www.elsa-vanier.fr
Hod, Paris: http://hod-boutique.com
IBU Gallery, Paris:
http://ibugallery.fr/gallery_en.html
L'Eclaireur, Paris: www.leclaireur.com
Le Bon Marché, Paris: www.lebonmarche.com
Le Royal Monceau (hotel shop), Paris:
www.leroyalmonceau.com
Lieu Commun, Paris: www.lieucommun.fr
Linea Chic (online shop): www.linea-chic.fr
Maria Luisa, Paris: www.marialuisa.fr
Matières à réflexion, Paris:
www.matieresareflexion.com
Merci, 111 boulevard Beaumarchais, 75003 Paris
Montaigne Market, Paris:
www.montaignemarket.com
Ostentatoire, Paris: www.ostentatoire-paris.com
Podium Jewellery, Paris and Courchevel:
www.podiumfashion.com
Surface to Air, Paris: www.surfacetoair.com
WHITE bIRD, Paris:
www.whitebirdjewellery.com

GERMANY
Andrea Schmidt, Dortmund:
www.gold-schmidt.de
Andreas Murkudis, Berlin:
www.andreasmurkudis.com
Artefakt, Munich: www.artefakt-muenchen.de
Darklands, Berlin: http://darklandsberlin.com
Edelschein, Berlin: www.edelschein.de
Frida, Frankfurt: www.frida-frankfurt.de
Grewenig Goldschmiede, Saarbrücken:
www.grewenig-goldschmiede.de
Jürgen Prüll, Weiden: www.pruell.de
My Theresa (online shop): www.mytheresa.com
Oona Gallery, Berlin: http://oona-galerie.de
Schmuckfrage, Berlin: www.schmuckfrage.de
Schmuckwelten, Galerie für Kunst & Design,
Pforzheim: www.schmuckwelten.de

HONG KONG
Harvey Nichols: www.harveynichols.com
Joyce: www.joyce.com
Lane Crawford: www.lanecrawford.com
On Pedder: www.onpedder.com

ITALY
10 Corso Como, Milan: www.10corsocomo.com
A Piedi Nudi nel Parco, Florence:
www.pnp-firenze.com

Antonioli, Milan and Turin: www.antonioli.eu
Le Noir, Cortina d'Ampezzo, Treviso and
Conegliano: www.lenoirboutique.it
Luisa Via Roma, Rome and Florence:
www.luisaviaroma.com
Penelope, Brescia: www.penelope-store.it
RUN in2 (online shop): www.runin2.com
Verdelilla, Turin: www.verdelilla.it

JAPAN
Baycrew's, Tokyo: www.baycrews.co.jp
Beams International Gallery, Tokyo:
www.beams.co.jp
Dover Street Market, Tokyo:
www.doverstreetmarket.com
GallardaGalante, Tokyo and other locations:
www.gallardagalante.com
Goldandbouncy, Tokyo:
http://goldandbouncy.com
Hankyu, Osaka: www.hankyu-dept.co.jp
HP France, Tokyo and Osaka: www.hpfrance.com
Isetan, Tokyo: www.isetan.co.jp
ISHIKIRI Village / ALAPHOLI, 5-4-54 Higashi
Ishikiri cyo, Higashi Osaka, Osaka
Lift, Tokyo: http://lift-net.co.jp
Loveless, Tokyo: www.loveless-shop.jp
Opening Ceremony, Tokyo:
www.openingceremonyjapan.com
Papillonner, Tokyo: www.papillonner-web.com
Restir, Tokyo: www.restir.com
SOSITE, Fukuoka and Tokyo:
http://sosites.wordpress.com
Spares, Fukuoka and Tokyo:
http://yokoou.wordpress.com
Strasburgo, Tokyo: www.strasburgo.co.jp
Super A Market, Tokyo: www.superamarket.jp
Tomorrowland, Tokyo: www.tomorrowland.co.jp
Trading Museum Comme des Garçons, Tokyo:
www.doverstreetmarket.com
United Arrows, Tokyo: www.united-arrows.co.jp
Via Bus Stop, Tokyo: www.viabusstop.com

KOREA
Boon The Shop, Seoul: www.boontheshop.com

KUWAIT
Octium Jewelry: www.octiumjewelry.com

LUXEMBOURG
Galerie Orfèo: www.galerie-orfeo.com

NETHERLANDS
Basalt, 's-Hertogenbosch: www.basaltdesign.nl
Cees de Vries edelsmid, Apeldoorn:
www.ceesdevriesedelsmid.nl

NEW ZEALAND
Clever Bastards (online shop):
www.cleverbastards.co.nz
Fingers, Auckland: www.fingers.co.nz
Form Gallery, Christchurch: www.form.co.nz

Quoil, Wellington: www.quoil.co.nz
SCOTTIES, Auckland and Wellington:
  http://scottiesboutique.co.nz

QATAR
The Vanity Room, Doha:
  http://thevanityroom.blogspot.com

ROMANIA
Entrance, Bucharest: www.entrance.ro

RUSSIA
DAYNIGHT, St Petersburg: www.day-night.ru
Golconda, Moscow: www.golconda.ru
Podium Concept Store, Moscow:
  www.podiumfashion.com
Project 3,14, Moscow:
  http://project314.blogspot.com
Tsum, Moscow: www.tsum.ru
Tsvetnoy Central Market, Moscow:
  www.tsvetnoy.com

SAUDI ARABIA
D'NA, Riyadh: www.dnariyadh.com
Harvey Nichols, Riyadh: www.harveynichols.com

SINGAPORE
Club 21: www.club21global.com
Front Row: www.frontrowsingapore.com
Hansel: www.ilovehansel.com
Les Amis: www.shoplesamis.com
Mardeu (online shop): www.mardeu.com

SPAIN
Ekseption, Madrid: www.ekseption.es
Fahoma, C/ Claudio Coello, 62, 28001 Madrid
Gallery Madrid: www.gallerymadrid.com
Klimt02 (online gallery): www.klimt02.net
Le Marché aux Puces, C/ Fernando VI, 2,
  28004 Madrid
MOTT, Madrid: www.mottmadrid.com
The Outpost, Barcelona:
  http://theoutpostbcn.com

SWITZERLAND
Goldschmiedeatelier Dominique Haefeli,
  Spalenberg 28, 4051 Basel
Jill Wolf, Geneva: www.jillwolfjewels.com
Schmuckschmiede Anja Camenzind, Brunnen:
  www.schmuckschmiedebrunnen.ch

TAIWAN
Club Designer: www.clubdesigner.com.tw

TURKEY
Beymen, Istanbul: www.beymen.com
Harvey Nichols, Ankara and Istanbul:
  www.harveynichols.com

UK
20ltd (online gallery): www.20ltd.com
Contemporary Applied Arts, London:
  www.caa.org.uk
CoutureLab, London: www.couturelab.com
Dark Room, London: www.darkroomlondon.com
Dover Street Market, London:
  www.doverstreetmarket.com
ECOne, London: www.econe.co.uk
Egg, London: http://eggtrading.eu

Electrum Gallery, London:
  www.electrumgallery.co.uk
Flow Gallery, London: www.flowgallery.co.uk
Harvey Nichols, London: www.harveynichols.com
Hervia Bazaar, Manchester: www.herviabazaar.com
Liberty, London: www.liberty.co.uk
Matches, London: www.matchesfashion.com
Mr Porter (online shop): www.mrporter.com
My Flash Trash (online shop):
  www.myflashtrash.com
My Wardrobe (online shop): www.my-wardrobe.com
Net-A-Porter (online shop): www.net-a-porter.com
Sweet Pea, London: http://sweetpeajewellery.com
Talisman Gallery, London:
  http://talismangallery.co.uk
The Convenience Store, London:
  http://theconveniencestorefashion.co.uk
The Shop at Bluebird, London:
  www.theshopatbluebird.com
Tom Dixon Showroom, 344 Ladbroke Grove,
  London W10 5BU

USA
Aaron Faber Gallery, New York:
  www.aaronfaber.com
ABC Home, New York: www.abchome.com
Adornments, Sag Harbor, NY:
  www.adornmentsfinejewelry.com
Alan Bilzerian, Boston: www.alanbilzerian.com
Alchemy, Portland, OR:
  www.alchemyjeweler.com
Artful Home (online shop): www.artfulhome.com
Barneys New York: www.barneys.com
Bergdorf Goodman, New York:
  www.bergdorfgoodman.com
BHLDN (online shop): www.bhldn.com
Blake, Chicago and Houston, 212 W. Chicago Ave.,
  Chicago, IL 60654
Charm & Chain (online shop):
  www.charmandchain.com
Church Boutique, Los Angeles:
  www.churchboutique.com
Curve, Los Angeles, New York, Miami and
  San Francisco: www.shopcurve.com
D&H Sustainable Jewelers, San Francisco:
  www.dnhjewelers.com
Egan Day, Philadelphia: www.eganday.com
Facéré, Seattle: www.facerejewelryart.com
FD, New York: http://fd-inspired.com
Gallery Loupe, Montclair, NJ:
  www.galleryloupe.com
Gallery of Jewels, San Francisco:
  www.galleryofjewels.com
Gladstone, Manchester by the Sea, MA:
  www.gladstonejewelry.com
Guild, Los Angeles: http://guildla.com
Gump's, San Francisco: www.gumps.com
Henri Bendel, New York: www.henribendel.com
Hummingbird Jewelers, Rhinebeck, NY:
  http://hummingbirdjewelers.com
IF, New York and Beirut, Lebanon:
  http://ifsohonewyork.com
Ikram, Chicago: http://ikram.com
Jeffrey, New York and Atlanta:
  http://jeffreynewyork.com
Jerry Szor, Dallas: www.jerryszor.com
Kirna Zabete, New York: www.kirnazabete.com
L-atitude (online shop): www.shoplatitude.com/
  shop-product/jewelry

Linda Dresner, Birmingham, MI:
  www.lindadresner.com
Love Adorned, New York: www.loveadorned.com
Marissa, Naples, FL: www.marissacollections.com
Maryam Nassir Zadeh, New York:
  www.mnzstore.com
Maxfield, Los Angeles: www.maxfieldla.com
Mazzarese, Leawood, KS: http://mazzarese.com
Meridian Jewelers, Aspen, CO:
  www.meridianjewelers.com
Mobilia Gallery, Cambridge, MA:
  http://mobilia-gallery.com
Neiman Marcus, New York:
  www.neimanmarcus.com
Opening Ceremony, New York and Los Angeles:
  www.openingceremony.us
Ornamentum, Hudson, NY:
  www.ornamentumgallery.com
Patron of the New, New York:
  http://patronofthenew.com
Paul Carter Jewels, Houston:
  http://new.paulcarterjewels.com
PEEL Gallery, Houston: www.peelgallery.org
Peggy Daven, Palm Beach, FL:
  www.peggydaven.com
Peipers & Kojen, 1023 Lexington Ave.,
  New York, NY 10021
Persimmon, Los Angeles:
  http://shoppersimmon.com
Reinhold Jewelers, Puerto Rico:
  www.reinholdjewelers.com
Robin Richman, Chicago:
  www.robinrichman.com
Roseark, West Hollywood and Santa Monica, CA:
  www.roseark.com
Sabbia, Chicago and Key Biscayne:
  http://sabbia.com
Scoop NYC, New York and other locations:
  www.scoopnyc.com
Shaw Jewelry, Northeast Harbor, MN:
  www.shawjewelry.com
Snyderman-Works Gallery, Philadelphia:
  www.snyderman-works.com
Sucre, New York: http://sucrenyc.com
Surface to Air, New York: www.surfacetoair.com
Susan, 1403 Burlingame Ave., Burlingame,
  CA 94010
Talavera by Aurora Lopez Mejia, New York:
  www.auroralopezmejia.com/talavera
Ted Muehling, New York: www.tedmuehling.com
The Clay Pot, Brooklyn, NY: www.clay-pot.com
The Store at the Museum of Arts and Design,
  New York: http://thestore.madmuseum.org
Treasure & Bond, New York:
  www.treasureandbond.com
Twist, Portland, OR: www.twistonline.com
Urban Flower Grange Hall, Dallas:
  www.urbanflowergrangehall.com
Velvet da Vinci, San Francisco:
  www.velvetdavinci.com
Ylang23, Dallas: www.ylang23.com
Zero + Maria Cornejo, New York and Los Angeles:
  http://zeromariacornejo.com

PICTURE CREDITS

a = above, b = below, c = centre, l = left, r = right

Image quality control – Helen Brooke www.maverickdesigntribe.com.au

Adeline Cacheux – pp. 108 al, 109 b courtesy of Adeline Cacheux; 108 ar & b, 109 a Mathieu Walter (www.mwgalerie.com); 108 cl & cr Laurent Deschamps (www.deschamps-laurent.com/advertising.html).

Akong – all photos courtesy of Akong.

Alexandra Jefford – all photos by Paul Bowden (www.paulbowden.co.uk), except for p. 134 b by Hassan Amini.

Alice Cicolini – pp. 76 a, cr & br, 77 al & ar Damon Cleary (damoncleary@hotmail.com); 76 cl, 77 b Nick Holt (www.nickholt.com).

Alina Alamorean – all photos by Ulysse Fréchelin (www.ulyssesworks.com), except for p. 50 b by Paola Sossou.

Alyssa Norton – pp. 110 a Michael Fox (www.michaeljamesfox.com); 110 b, 111 al & br, 288 Jessica Antola (www.antolaphoto.com); 111 ar & bl Josh Ponte.

Andy Lifschutz – pp. 54 Nialls Fallon (www.niallsfallon.com); 55 a Rudolf Bekker (http://rudolfbekker.com); 55 b Tyler Kohlhoff (www.tylerkohlhoff.com).

Anndra Neen – all photos by Jon Kamantigue (www.fotokoto.com), except for p. 56 b courtesy of Anndra Neen.

Anne Zellien – all photos by Stany Dederen (www.dederen.be).

Annie Costello Brown – all photos by Zen Sekizawa (http://zensekizawa.com), except for p. 194 b by Jeaneen Lund (http://jeaneenlund.com).

Anton Heunis – all photos by Thomas Laubscher (www.laubscher.de), except for p. 13 b courtesy of Anton Heunis.

Apriati – pp. 112 al & b, 113 a Vassilis Michail (www.vmichail.eu); 112 ar, 113 c Alexandros Botonakis (botonaki@acsmi.gr); 113 b courtesy of Apriati.

Assad Mounser – all photos courtesy of Henry Mounser Photography (www.henrymounser.com).

Aude Lechère – all photos by Thomas Goldet.

Belmacz – pp. 136 Franck Allais (www.franckallais.com); 137 al & ar, 138, 139 a Ryan Davies; 137 b Robert Rowland (www.robert-rowland.com); 139 c & b Holger Pooten (www.holgerpooten.com).

Benedikt von Lepel – all photos by Peter Falkner (www.peterfalknerphoto.com), except for p. 168 bl by Luca Nicolao (www.lucanicolao.com).

Bijules – all photos by Thomas Liggett (http://thomasliggett.com).

Bliss Lau – pp. 198 al, ar & br, 199 al & ar Jarrod Turner (http://jarrodturner.com); 198 bl Eric Guillemain (www.ericguillemain.com); 199 b Robyn Twomey (www.robyntwomey.com).

Catherine Michiels – all photos courtesy of Catherine Michiels.

Cathy Waterman – all photos by Gretchen Bayer (www.thesnapshotist.com), except for p. 220 a courtesy of Cathy Waterman.

CCCHU – all photos courtesy of CCCHU.

Cristina Zazo – all photos by Raúl Córdoba (www.raulcordobaphotography.com), except for p. 170 b courtesy of Cristina Zazo.

Culoyon – all photos courtesy of Culoyon.

Darcy Miro – pp. 58 a, cl & bl Tim Thayer; 58 br, 59 a Elizabeth Waugh (www.elizabethwaughphotography.com); 59 b Amber Rima (www.amberrimaphoto.com).

Deborah Pagani – all photos courtesy of Deborah Pagani.

Delphine-Charlotte Parmentier – all photos courtesy of Qwark - Delphine-Charlotte Parmentier.

Du Poil de la Bête – all photos courtesy of Du Poil de la Bête, except for p. 18 b Lou Sarda (http:// lousarda.tumblr.com).

Eddie Borgo – all photos courtesy of Eddie Borgo.

Eleanor Ford – all photos courtesy of Eleanor Ford.

Elena Votsi – all photos courtesy of Elena Votsi.

Esther – pp. 116 a Adrien Alleaume (http://adrien_alleaume.ultra-book.com/portfolio); 116 b, 117 al & ar Gwenaelle Dautricourt; 117 b courtesy of Esther Assouline.

Eva Steinberg – all photos by Matthias Demand (www.demandlichtbilder.de), except for p. 82 ar by Dieter Wagner.

Fabien Ifires – all photos courtesy of Fabien Ifires.

Fanourakis – pp. 224 a, 226 br, 227 cr Panagiotis Baxevanis (www.fantasticamera.com); 224 b, 226 al & ar, 227 a & b Anestis Kyriakidis (http://graphicon.gr); 225, 226 bl, 227 cl Yorgos Yerardos (www.yorgos yerardos.com).

Farrah Al-Dujaili – all photos courtesy of Farrah Al-Dujaili; model Sarah Green.

Fiona Paxton – pp. 2, 26 ar & bl, 27 courtesy of Fiona Paxton; 26 al & br Henrik Adamsen (www.henrikadamsen.com); model Elise at Unique.

Frances Wadsworth-Jones – pp. 174, 175 al & bl courtesy of Frances Wadsworth-Jones; 175 ar Dominic Tschudin; 175 c & br RJ Fernandez (www.shootrj.com).

Ginger McGann – pp. 28 al, 29 Kim Sehyung (Studio AJ9); 28 ar & bl courtesy of Ginger McGann.

Glauco Cambi – all photos courtesy of Frameout Photo by Serafino Di Gregorio (www.frameout.it).

Gonzague Zurstrassen – pp. 228 a, 229 al, bl & br, 230, 231 courtesy of Gonzague Zurstrassen; 228 b Soneva Kiri by Six Senses (www.sixsenses.com/Soneva-Kiri); 229 ar Benya Hegenbarth (www.benyahegenbarth.com).

Hannah Martin – all photos by Chris Peun (www.chrispeun.com), except for p. 144 b courtesy of Hannah Martin Ltd.

Hanut Singh – all photos by Sarabjit Babra (www.darirc.com), except for p. 233 b courtesy of Hanut Singh.

Heaven Tanudiredja – all photos by Zeb Daemen (www.zebdaemen.com); model Feline Visscher at Paparazzi Amsterdam, Storm London, Women Management Milan and Paris.

Inez Designs – all photos by Ben Siow (www.abundant-productions.com).

Isabel Dammermann – all photos by Federico Cavicchioli (federico@prodigo.de).

JACCO – all photos by Jean-François Julian (http:// iloveyoutous.blogspot.com).

Jacqueline Rabun – all photos by Tom Brown (http://thomasbrown.info), except for p. 146 b by Annabel Elston (http://bird-production.com/Artists/AE/AE_Portfolio.html).

Jacquie Aiche – all photos by Laura Layera (www.luluphoto.com), except for p. 118 b by Naj Jamaï (www.najjamai.com).

Jennifer Trask – pp. 264 courtesy of Jennifer Trask; 265 a Dmitri Belyi (www.dmitribelyi.com); 265 b Robert Hansen-Sturm (www.stormphotoinc.com).

Jessica McCormack – all photos by Jasper Gough, except for p. 237 a by David Yeo (www.davidyeo.co.uk).

Julia deVille – all photos by Terence Bogue (http://tbogue.com), except for p. 200 a by James Geer (www.jamesgeer.com).

Karen Liberman – all photos by Emmanuel Santos (http://web.mac.com/etsantos/etsantos/Emmanuel_Santos.html).

Katey Brunini – pp. 238 al Alexandra Zousmer (www.kbrunini.com); 238 ar, 239 bl & br Chris Trayer (www.christrayer.com); 238 b Visko Hatfield (www.vhpictures.com); 239 a Peter Hurst.

Kimberlin Brown – pp. 84, 85 al Stuart Tyson (http://stuarttysonphoto.com); 85 ar & br Dag Bennstrom (www.dagomatic.net).

kwodrent – pp. 266 a courtesy of kwodrent; 266 bl, 267 Caleb Ming (www.surround.sg); 266 bc & br Darren Soh (www.darrensoh.com).

Lady Grey – all photos by Greg Vore (www.greg vore.com), except for p. 205 b by Sunny Shokrae (http://sunnyshokrae.com).

Lara Melchior – all photos courtesy of Lara Melchior.

Laurent Gandini – all photos by Orlando Salmeri (www.orlandosalmeri.com), except for p. 86 b Cristina Costantini.

Le Buisson – all photos by Pierre Mendelssohn, courtesy of Le Buisson, except for p. 149 b by Matali Crasset, courtesy of Le Buisson.

Lia di Gregorio – all photos by Carlo Lavatori (www.carlolavatori.com), except for p. 89 br courtesy of Lia di Gregorio.

Lisa Cooper – pp. 268 a Tania Kelley (www.tania kelley.com) / Cate Blanchett and Peter Carroll in Sydney Theatre Company production, *The War of the Roses*, 2009; 268 b, 269 al, ar & bl Eliza Gorka (http://tb060.blogspot.com); 269 br Samuel Hodge (http://truth-beauty-cock.blogspot.com) / stylist Jolyon Mason (www.2c.com.au/artist. cfm?ArtistID=85).

Lito Karakostanoglou – all photos by Ulysse Fréchelin (www.ulyssesworks.com), except for p. 240 b by Alexandre Tsipouridis (http:// tsipouridis.net).

Lizzie Fortunato Jewels – pp. 36 al, 37 al & br Jason Ross Savage (www.collectiveedit.com); 36 b Mike Vorrasi (www.vorrasi.com); 37 ar & bl Kfir Ziv (www.kfirziv.com).

Louise Douglas – all photos courtesy of Louise Douglas.

Lucifer Vir Honestus – all photos courtesy of Lucifer Vir Honestus.

Manya & Roumen – pp. 176 a & br Hap Sakwa (www.hapsakwa.com); 176 c & bl, 177 al & b Chris Trayer (www.christrayer.com); 177 ar courtesy of Manya Tessler.

Marc Alary – all photos courtesy of Marc Alary.

Margery Hirschey – all photos courtesy of Margery Hirschey, except for p. 90 ar by John Sandhu.

Massimo Izzo – all photos by Enrico Ummarino (www.ummarinoeummarino.com), except for p. 247 b by Catalina Muñoz.

Melanie Georgacopoulos – all photos by Jeremy Johns (www.jeremyjohns.co.uk), except for p. 151 b courtesy of Melanie Georgacopoulos.

Michelle Lowe-Holder – pp. 7, 270, 272 Polly Penrose (www.pollypenrose.com); 271 courtesy of Michelle Lowe-Holder, painting by Jon Waldo (www.jonwaldo.com); 273 Ines Gomes.

Molayem – all photos by Antonio Barrella (www.studiorizzonte.com).

Mouton Collet – all photos courtesy of Mouton Collet.

Natalie Frigo – all photos by Ken Kronus (www.kronusphoto.com).

Nicola Malkin – pp. 274 courtesy of Nicola Malkin; 275 al & ar Steve Laverty; 275 b Tyrone Lebon.

Nicole Landaw – all photos by RSP Media (http://rspmedia.com), except for p. 95 ar by David S. Brown (www.dsbphotography.com).

Nuit N°12 – all photos by Serge Paulet (www. sergepaulet.com), except for p. 206 ar by Pierre Gayte (http://pierregayte.free.fr).

Pamela Love – pp. 64 a courtesy of Pamela Love; 64 b, 65 Marco Pedde (www.marcopedde.com); 65 bl Ian Roberts (http://ianswork.com); 66, 67 Adrian Gaut (www.agaut.com).

Pat Falcão – all photos by Patricia Ikeda (www.patriciaikeda.com.br).

Patricia Madeja – all photos by Ken Cox (www.kronusphoto.com), except for p. 155 b by Steph Mantis (www.stephmantis.com).

Paula Bianco – all photos by Alex Pergament.

Percossi Papi – all photos by Edmondo Angelelli (www.studiooctopus.it), except for p. 251 b by Barry Michlin (www.barrymichlin.com).

Petra Class – all photos by Hap Sakwa (www. hapsakwa.com), except for p. 96 b Anne Hamersky (www.annehamersky.com).

Philippa Holland – all photos by Rama Lee (www.ramagraphy.com), except for p. 184 b courtesy of Philippa Holland Fine Jewellery.

Philippe Cramer – all photos by Marian Gérard (www.studio-gerard.ch), except for p. 156 ar courtesy of Philippe Cramer.

RedSofa by Joanna Szkiela – all photos by Anthony McLean, except for p. 69 b Jane Heller (www.janehellerphotography.com).

Regina Dabdab – pp. 208 a, 209 ar & bl Roberta Dabdab (http://robertadabdab.com); 208 b Poul Ober (www.poulober.com); 209 al & br Henrike Stahl (www.henrikestahl.de).

RP/Encore – all photos by Tom Houser (http:// tomhouser.co.uk), except for p. 211 a by Felicity Ieraci (http://felicityjade.wordpress.com).

Russell Jones – pp. 98, 99 al & br, 100 Elizabeth Waugh (www.elizabethwaughphotography.com); 99 ar Matthew Sussman (www.matthewsussman. com); 101 Kyle Mix (www.1009photography.com).

Sabina Kasper – all photos courtesy of Sabina Kasper.

SAMMA – all photos courtesy of Hanna Sandin.

Sibylle Krause – all photos by Petra Jaschke, except for p. 159 b courtesy of Sibylle Krause.

Silke Knetsch & Christian Streit – all photos by Rainer Muranyi (www.rainermuranyi.de).

Sophia 203 – all photos by Jonas Spinoy (http://fatafatphoto.blogspot.com).

Spreeglanz – pp. 276 a courtesy of Cherry Boonyapan; 276 b Peter Lorenz (http:// petetheheat.com/index.php?/peter-lorenz/); 277 Elena Busshoff (www.elenabusshoff.de).

Stacy Hopkins – all photos by Charley Freiberg (http://charleyfreibergphotography.com).

Stephanie Simon – pp. 190 al & br, 191 b John Ross; 190 ar & bl, 191 al Tony Cordoza (www.tonycordoza.com); 191 ar Katrina Baer.

Stone - all photos by Nicolas Gaillard (http:// nicolasgaillard.com), except for p. 128 b courtesy of Stone.

Sylvie Corbelin – all photos courtesy of Sylvie Corbelin.

Tobias Wistisen – all photos by Christophe Sion (www.christophe-sion.com).

Todd Reed – all photos courtesy of Todd Reed.

uncommon matters – pp. 278 al & br, 279 b Martin Thacker; 278 ar & bl Mark Pillai (www.markpillai.com); 279 a Maximilian Rossner (www.maximilianrossner.de); model Suzanna at Elite Paris.

Unearthen – all photos by Zen Sekizawa (http://zensekizawa.com).

Ursa Major – pp. 130 al & br, 131 b Ellinor Stigle (http://ellinorstigle.com); 130 ar, cl & bl Lahaina Alcantara for Love Adorned (http:// lahainaalcantara.com); 131 b Lenard Smith (www.lenardsmith.com).

Venessa Arizaga – all photos by Shawn Roche (www.shawnrochephoto.com), except for p. 45 b Joseph D'Arco (http://fotodarco.com).

Victoria Simes – pp. 280 a, 281, 282 c & b, 283 Roderick Angle (www.roderickangle.com); 280 b Daniel Holguin (www.multiplicities.info); 282 a Ernesto Gonzales (www.ernestogonzalez. com); model Janelle Fishman.

Yatüz – pp. 254 a & cl Sham Hinchey and Marzia Messina (www.marshamstreet.com); 254 cr & b, 255 al & ar Riccardo Cavallari and Nayla El Amin (www.cavallari.co.uk); 255 b Taro Di Fabio.

Yunus & Eliza – all photos by Drew Cox (http://drewcox.co.uk), except for p. 160 b by Saulo Jamariqueli (http://nearlynormal.tv/ saulojamariqueli).

OVERLEAF One-of-a-kind necklace by Alyssa Norton, 1940s vintage rhinestones and woven hand-dyed silk, *SS12* collection.

ACKNOWLEDGMENTS

Thank you! To all the designers
who accepted my invitation to participate
in this book. Despite distance, you
opened your fascinating world to me and I can now
enthusiastically share it with a wider audience.
Your talent and discerning creativity will always amaze me.
To the committed people, who, through their dedication in
supporting jewelers, have shared their experience with me: Béatrice
Saint-Laurent (Galerie BSL), Stéphanie Roger (White Bird fine jewelry
boutique) and Valery Demure (VALERYdemure creative agency).
To all the publishing staff involved in the process of making this book happen,
in particular Karolina Prymaka. And lastly to my dearest ones:
Marie-Françoise, André, Christine, Mark, Ludivine, Pierre and Helen.
My gratitude, in carat terms, would probably surpass
the biggest gem ever found.

ABOUT THE AUTHOR

Olivier Dupon began his career at Christian Dior. He expanded his
expertise in the fields of fashion and lifestyle by working as a buyer
and product manager for several large retail companies before opening
his own boutique. Based in Australia, he now scouts international
markets in search of design/art/craft objects and projects
to feature on his blog, www.Dossier37.tumblr.com.
His previous book, *The New Artisans*, was published
by Thames & Hudson in 2011. His new book
on pâtisserie will be published in 2013.